*Penguin Books*

*The British in Love*

Jilly Cooper was born in Essex in 1937 and had nearly twenty-five jobs before she was given a column in the *Sunday Times*. She has written nineteen books and nine television plays and lives in London with a large husband, two children, three dogs and a floating population of cats. She lists her hobbies as French Literature and matching mongrels.

# The British in Love

## Jilly Cooper

Penguin Books

♥

Penguin Books Ltd, Harmondsworth,
Middlesex, England
Penguin Books, 625 Madison Avenue,
New York, New York 10022, U.S.A.
Penguin Books Australia Ltd, Ringwood,
Victoria, Australia
Penguin Books Canada Ltd, 2801 John Street,
Markham, Ontario, Canada L3R 1B4
Penguin Books (N.Z.) Ltd, 182–190 Wairau Road,
Auckland 10, New Zealand

First published by Arlington Books 1980
Published in Penguin Books 1981

Typeset, printed and bound in Great Britain by
Hazell Watson & Viney Ltd,
Aylesbury, Bucks
Set in Intertype Lectura

*To Aphra Lloyd,*
*with love and gratitude*

# Contents

# Acknowledgements

Grateful thanks are due to the following publishers and copyright holders for permission to reprint the extracts which appear in this book:

Barbara Pym and Jonathan Cape Ltd for *A Glass of Blessings*; the estate of C. Day Lewis, Jonathan Cape Ltd and the Hogarth Press for *The Album* from *Collected Poems 1954*; E. S. Duckworth for *Juliet* and *The False Heart* by Hilaire Belloc, and *Three Weeks* by Elinor Glyn; the Society of Authors as the literary representative of the Estate of A. E. Housman, and Jonathan Cape Ltd for A. E. Housman's *Collected Poems*; Barrie & Jenkins for the extract from *Uneasy Money* by P. G. Wodehouse; Macmillan and Company Ltd and Michael and Anne Yeats for *Down by the Salley Gardens, Never Give All the Heart, The Pity of Love, The Falling of the Leaves* and *The Folly of Being Comforted* by W. B. Yeats; Douglas Sutherland for the extract from *The English Gentleman*; Pan Books Ltd for *Celia Celia* by Adrian Mitchell and the Chaucer modernization on page 68 by Alan Bold, which appear in *Making Love: The Picador Book of Erotic Verse* edited by Alan Bold; Laurence Pollinger Ltd and the estate of the late Mrs Frieda Lawrence Ravagli for *To a Young Wife* by D. H. Lawrence; Methuen Children's Books Ltd for *Disobedience* by A. A. Milne which appears in *When We Were Very Young*; Faber and Faber Ltd for *The Double Shame* from *Collected Poems by Stephen Spender, A Dedication to My Wife, Ash Wednesday* and *The Cocktail Party* from *Collected Poems 1909–1962* and *The Cocktail Party* by T. S. Eliot, *Song* and *Who's Who* from *Collected Poems* of W. H. Auden and *Johnny* from *The English Auden* by W. H. Auden, *Sonnet to My Mother* by George Barker from *Collected Poems 1930–1955, Les Sylphides* by Louis MacNeice from *Collected Poems of Louis MacNeice*; the *Daily Mirror* for *The Duck Walk* by Keith Waterhouse; William Heinemann for *The Acceptance World* by Anthony Powell;

Hamish Hamilton Ltd for *Love in a Cold Climate* by Nancy Mitford and *Passion* by Kathleen Raine; the *Sunday Express* for the extract by Nathaniel Gubbins; Roger McGough for *At Lunchtime A Story of Love*; André Deutsch Ltd for *Guarantee* by Philip Oakes; A. D. Peters & Company Ltd for *Diary of a Provincial Lady* by E. M. Delafield and *First Love* by Gerald Bullett; Macmillan Administration (Basingstoke) Ltd for *At Castle Boterel*, *A Thunderstorm in Town*, *I Look Into My Glass* and *In the Time of 'the Breaking of Nations'* by Thomas Hardy; John Murray (Publishers) Ltd for *Indoor Games near Newbury*, *Lenten Thoughts of a High Anglican*, *Pot Pourri From A Surrey Garden*, *Agricultural Caress*, *In a Bath Teashop*, *Business Girls* and *A Subaltern's Love Song* by John Betjeman from *Collected Poems of John Betjeman*; Robert Graves for *Symptoms of Love* and *O Love in Me*; Edinburgh University Press for *Strawberries* by Edwin Morgan; George Allen & Unwin for *Weddings* by A. P. Herbert and *Party Piece* by Brian Patten, A. P. Watt for the extract from *The History of Mr Polly* by H. G. Wells; and Merlin Holland and Oxford University Press for two letters by Oscar Wilde.

The author and publisher have taken all possible care to trace the ownership of all works in copyright reprinted in this book, and to make acknowledgement for their use. If any omissions have accidentally occurred, they will be corrected in subsequent editions, provided notification is sent to the publisher.

My thanks are also due to Mrs Beryl Hill for typing the manuscript so beautifully, to Miss Maxine Green for collecting the permissions, and to my publishers for producing such an elegant book.

# Introduction

I suppose the ultimate ego trip, after going on *Desert Island Discs*, is to be asked to compile an anthology of your favourite poetry and prose. This happened to me last year when David Heycock, a producer for BBC 2, commissioned me to choose material and write the linking passages for a programme called *The British in Love*. There were only two strictures: the material must deal with some aspect of romantic love, and it must have been written by English, Scottish, Welsh or Irish authors.

Having been steeped in literature since I was five, I found the problem was not what to put in, but what on earth to leave out. My grandfather, for example, could quote most of Shakespeare, and frequently did. My mother and my grandmother read everything they could get their hands on. My aunt wrote poetry which actually got published. My father, having been to Rugby, was addicted to the Rugby poets, and would reel off Matthew Arnold, Rupert Brooke or Henry Newbolt at every opportunity.

Literature, however, was not taken over-seriously in our household. My Great-Uncle Alec, for example, the family punner, once visited Liverpool. Standing on the quayside, peering down at the dirty, rubbish-clogged river, he cried out:

'The quality of Mersey is not strained.'

One of my favourite poems as a teenager was Keats' sonnet about Stout Cortez staring with eagle eyes at the Pacific, 'silent upon a peak in Darien'. My father one day pointed out that the peak could have been a pekinese. From then onwards I had this picture of a poor dog flattened beneath some overweight and contemplative pioneer. Our next-door neighbour had a ginger cat called Hopkins; after it was neutered my brother called it Gerard Unmanly. So ours was not the sort of atmosphere in which poetic natures flourished.

At school, however, I was lucky enough to have a marvellous English mistress. Tall, dark, with snapping black eyes, a cackling laugh and a dramatic dress sense, she seemed to fill the dusty classrooms with light. Under her inspired and fiery guidance, many of the great characters in literature – Viola, Henry Esmond, the Mayor of Casterbridge, Sir Roger de Coverley – came permanently to life. So good was her training that after I left school and worked on a local paper, I never went anywhere without clutching some volume of poetry, which doubled up as a reporter's notebook. To this day, in my copy of *The Wreck of the Deutschland* are scribbled the shorthand details of a scrap metal theft. While underneath Auden's poem about Verlaine and Rimbaud is scrawled a policeman's evidence in court:

'As I was proceeding along the footway, I saw the defendant sitting in the gutter, he said "I am Humpty Dumpty, I bet you can't put me together again", and I formed the opinion he was drunk.'

Always a compulsive prose reader, I suppose poetry appealed to me most between the ages of 14 and 24, when I was desperately searching for a permanent mate, and ricochetting from one disastrous boyfriend to another. Only in poetry could I find appropriate expression for my ecstasy when things were going right, or despair when things went wrong:

> *He's* gone, *he's* gone; when thou know'st this,
> Thou know'st how dry a cinder this world is.

Even when I found real love and got married, I still went on reading and taking a passionate interest in my friends' love affairs, filling as I went along endless notebooks with fragments of poetry and prose that appealed to me.

Consequently, when I came to compile *The British in Love* for the BBC as a St Valentine's Day celebration, I found there was enough for at least half a dozen programmes. So my publisher, Desmond Elliott, suggested I should collect all the material into this book.

The result is a very personal collection, almost an autobiography of love. I start with the first tentative steps towards a relationship, move on to the traumas of love and loss, through engagements, marriage successful and unsuccessful, adultery, old age and death.

One of the nice things about poetry is that it brings people together. While I was collecting material, my BBC producer, David Heycock, also a poetry fanatic, introduced me to several poems: Edwin Morgan's *Strawberries*, *A Shilling Life* by Auden, which I liked so much I included them in the anthology.

But principally it is a collection of old friends who have beguiled, comforted, and amused me over the years.

'For poetry makes nothing happen,' wrote Auden.

> It flows south
> From ranches of isolation and the busy griefs,
> Raw towns that we believe and die in; it survives,
> A way of happening, a mouth.

And Auden is right. Literature may not change the world, but it survives because, by identifying with our happiness or our suffering, it makes us feel we are not alone.

And if anyone gets a quarter of the pleasure reading this book that I have had compiling it, I shall be very happy.

Jilly Cooper, 1980

# First Love

We are first aware of love when we realize we are dependent on someone else for our happiness. A child's first love is usually for one of its parents. I hero-worshipped my father. My adoration reached its height towards the end of the last war when he became one of the youngest Brigadiers in the army, which appealed to my snobbish instincts, even at the age of five. He had brilliant delphinium blue eyes, and was tall, with very broad shoulders. When I saw him coming home down the street in his uniform with that brisk, swinging, ramrod-backed, military walk, I used nearly to faint with pride.

Most boys, on the other hand, tend to adore their mothers, a passion they often never grow out of – as many women know to their cost. Here three poets remember their mothers in very different ways. William Cowper's portrait, though charming, seems almost too idealistic. Could his mother have been that loving all the time? One suspects there was a good nanny doing all the heavy work, leaving Mrs Cowper smilingly free to hand out sugar plums, make paper flowers, and bestow tender goodnight kisses. George Barker's mother – vast, merry, gin-swilling – seems far more human. I love the image of young George trailing after her like a little dog following a brass band. James James Morrison's mother, however, seems a cross between the two, radiantly beautiful but somewhat louche in behaviour. The fact that she was sneaking off to the end of the town in a gold dress and vowing to be back by tea-time suggests she was up to a liquid lunch at the least.

Where once we dwelt our name is heard no more,
Children not thine have trod my nurs'ry floor;
And where the gard'ner Robin, day by day,

Drew me to school along the public way,
Delighted with my bauble coach, and wrapp'd
In scarlet mantle warm, and velvet capt,
'Tis now become a hist'ry little known,
That once we call'd the past'ral house our own.
Short-liv'd possession! but the record fair,
That mem'ry keeps of all thy kindness there,
Still outlives many a storm, that has effac'd
A thousand other themes less deeply trac'd.
Thy nightly visits to my chamber made,
That thou might'st know me safe and warmly laid;
Thy morning bounties ere I left my home,
The biscuit, or confectionary plum;
The fragrant waters on my cheeks bestow'd
By thy own hand, till fresh they shone and glow'd:
All this, and more endearing still than all,
Thy constant flow of love, that knew no fall,
Ne'er roughen'd by those cataracts and breaks,
That humour interpos'd too often makes;
All this still legible in mem'ry's page,
And still to be so to my latest age,
Adds joy to duty, makes me glad to pay
Such honours to thee as my numbers may;
Perhaps a frail memorial, but sincere,
Not scorn'd in heav'n, though little notic'd here.
    Could Time, his flight revers'd, restore the hours,
When, playing with thy vesture's tissu'd flow'rs —
The violet, the pink, and jessamine —
I prick'd them into paper with a pin,
(And thou wast happier than myself the while,
Wouldst softly speak, and stroke my head, and smile)
Could those few pleasant hours again appear,
Might one wish bring them, would I wish them here?
I would not trust my heart — the dear delight
Seems so to be desir'd, perhaps I might. —
But no — what here we call our life is such,
So little to be lov'd and thou so much,

That I should ill requite thee to constrain
Thy unbound spirit into bonds again.

from *On the Receipt of My Mother's Picture
out of Norfolk*, William Cowper

Most near, most dear, most loved and most far,
Under the window where I often found her
Sitting as huge as Asia, seismic with laughter,
Gin and chicken helpless in her Irish hand,
Irresistible as Rabelais, but most tender for
The lame dogs and hurt birds that surround her, —
She is a procession no one can follow after
But be like a little dog following a brass band.
She will not glance up at the bomber or condescend
To drop her gin and scuttle to a cellar,
But lean on the mahogany table like a mountain
Whom only faith can move, and so I send
O all my faith and all my love to tell her
That she will move from mourning into morning.

*Sonnet to My Mother*, George Barker

James James
Morrison Morrison
Weatherby George Dupree
Took great
Care of his Mother
Though he was only three.
James James
Said to his Mother,
'Mother,' he said, said he:
'You must never go down to the end of the town,
  if you don't go down with me.'

James James
Morrison's Mother
Put on a golden gown,
James James

Morrison's Mother
Drove to the end of the town.
James James
Morrison's Mother
Said to herself, said she:
'I can get right down to the end of the town
    and be back in time for tea.'

King John
Put up a notice,
'LOST or STOLEN or STRAYED!
JAMES JAMES
MORRISON'S MOTHER
SEEMS TO HAVE BEEN MISLAID.
LAST SEEN
WANDERING VAGUELY:
QUITE OF HER OWN ACCORD,
SHE TRIED TO GET DOWN TO THE END OF
    THE TOWN — FORTY SHILLINGS REWARD!'

James James
Morrison Morrison
(Commonly known as Jim)
Told his
Other relations
Not to go blaming *him*.
James James
*Said* to his Mother,
'Mother,' he said, said he:
'You must *never* go down to the end of the town
    without consulting me.'

James James
Morrison's mother
Hasn't been heard of since.
King John
Said he was sorry,
So did the Queen and Prince.

King John
(Somebody told me)
Said to a man he knew:
'If people go down to the end of the town, well,
    what can *anyone* do?'

(*Now then, very softly*)
J.J.
M.M.
W.G. du P.
Took great
C/o his M*****
Though he was only 3.
J.J.
Said to his M*****
'M*****,' he said, said he:
'You-must-never-go-down-to-the-end-of-the-town-
    if-you-don't-go-down-with ME!'

*Disobedience*, A. A. Milne

*Some children fall tenderly in love with other children. I myself
would have been far too tomboyish and keen on ponies and
dogs to attract the shy little boy at John Betjeman's children's
party. Wendy, however, was different.*

In among the silver birches winding ways of tarmac wander
    And the signs to Bussock Bottom, Tussock Wood and
        Windy Brake,
Gabled lodges, tile-hung churches, catch the lights of our
        Lagonda
    As we drive to Wendy's party, lemon curd and Christmas
        cake.

Rich the makes of motor whirring,
Past the pine-plantation purring
    Come up, Hupmobile, Delage!
Short the way your chauffeurs travel,

Crunching over private gravel
  Each from out his warm garáge.

Oh but Wendy, when the carpet yielded to my indoor pumps
  There you stood, your gold hair streaming,
  Handsome in the hall-light gleaming
There you looked and there you led me off into the game of
    clumps.

Then the new Victrola playing
And your funny uncle saying
'Choose your partners for a fox-trot! Dance until it's *tea*
    o'clock!
  'Come on, young 'uns, foot it featly!'
  Was it chance that paired us neatly,
  I, who loved you so completely,
You, who pressed me closely to you, hard against your party
    frock?

'Meet me when you've finished eating!' So we met and no
    one found us.
  Oh that dark and furry cupboard while the rest played hide
    and seek!
Holding hands our two hearts beating in the bedroom silence
    round us,
  Holding hands and hardly hearing sudden footsteps, thud
    and shriek.

Love that lay too deep for kissing —
'Where is Wendy? Wendy's missing!'
  Love so pure it *had* to end,
Love so strong that I was frighten'd
When you gripped my fingers tight and
Hugging, whispered 'I'm your friend.'

Goodbye Wendy! Send the fairies, pinewood elf and larch tree
    gnome,
  Spingle-spangled stars are peeping
  At the lush Lagonda creeping

Down the winding ways of tarmac to the leaded lights of
    home.

    There, among the silver birches,
    All the bells of all the churches
Sounded in the bath-waste running out into the frosty air.
    Wendy speeded my undressing,
    Wendy is the sheet's caressing
    Wendy bending gives a blessing,
Holds me as I drift to dreamland, safe inside my slumberwear.

*Indoor Games near Newbury*, John Betjeman

*For me, love first struck at the age of eleven, when I fell like a
log for one of the school prefects, who played third man at
lacrosse and looked like the young Churchill. How chastely and
undemandingly I adored her, giving her my sweet ration every
month, filling her locker with bluebells in the summer and
hazel nuts in the autumn. One of the characteristics of first
love is its humility. A word or a nod of recognition would keep
me going for days.*

Pray but one prayer for me 'twixt thy closed lips,
    Think but one thought of me up in the stars.
The summer night waneth, the morning light slips,
    Faint and grey 'twixt the leaves of the aspen, betwixt the
        cloud bars,
That are patiently waiting there for the dawn:
    Patient and colourless, though Heaven's gold
Waits to float through them alone with the sun.
Far out in the meadows, above the young corn,
    The heavy elms wait, and restless and cold
The uneasy wind rises; the roses are dun;
Through the long twilight they pray for the dawn,
Round the lone house in the midst of the corn.
    Speak but one word to me over the corn,
    Over the tender, bow'd locks of the corn.

*Summer Dawn*, William Morris

*Another feature of first love is the desire to be of use to the beloved. Here, first, we see poor Caliban, his brain befuddled by drinking, offering his services to the brutish Stephano; and, secondly, Gerald Bullett's schoolboy similarly poleaxed by an older woman:*

I'll show thee the best springs: I'll pluck thee berries;
I'll fish for thee, and get thee wood enough . . .
I prithee let me bring thee where crabs grow
And I with my long nails will dig thee pig nuts,
Show thee a jay's nest and instruct thee how
To snare the nimble marmozet; I'll bring thee
To clust'ring filberts, and sometimes I'll get thee
Young scamels from the rock. Wilt thou go with me?

from *The Tempest*,
William Shakespeare


When I was in my fourteenth year,
And captain of the third eleven,
I fell in love with Guenevere,
And hovered at the gate of heaven.
She wasn't more than twenty-seven.

I partnered her, by happy chance,
At tennis, losing every game.
No shadow dimmed her careless glance,
No teasing word, no hint of blame.
Brightlier burned my secret flame.

Nothing I asked but to adore,
In dumb surrender, shy and stiff:
But ah, she gave me how much more,
A benison beyond belief!
'Just hold my racquet for a jiff.'

*First Love*, Gerald Bullett

*The romantic, of course, are always in love from 'kiddie-car to hearse' as Fanny, a young girl, explains to two older women, Lady Montdore and Mrs Chaddesley Corbett:*

'Come over here, Fanny.'

I was almost too much surprised to be alarmed by this summons and hurried over, wondering what it could all be about.

'Sit there,' she said, pointing to a needle-work chair, 'and talk to us. Are you in love?'

I felt myself becoming scarlet in the face. How could they have guessed my secret? Of course I had been in love for two days now, ever since my morning walk with the Duc de Sauveterre. Passionately, but as indeed I realized, hopelessly, in love. In fact, the very thing that Lady Montdore had intended for Polly had befallen me.

'There you are, Sonia,' said Mrs Chaddesley Corbett triumphantly, tapping a cigarette with nervous violence against her jewelled case and lighting it with a gold lighter, her pale blue eyes never meanwhile leaving my face. 'What did I tell you? Of course she is, poor sweet, just look at that blush, it must be something quite new and horribly bogus. I know, it's my dear old husband. Confess, now! I couldn't mind less, actually.'

I did not like to say that I still, after a whole week-end, had no idea at all which of the many husbands present hers might be, but stammered out as quickly as I could.

'Oh no no, not anybody's husband, I promise. Only a fiancé, and such a detached one at that.'

They both laughed.

'All right,' said Mrs Chaddesley Corbett, 'we're not going to worm. What we really want to know, to settle a bet, is, have you always fancied somebody ever since you can remember? Answer truthfully, please.'

I was obliged to admit that this was the case. From a tiny child, ever since I could remember, in fact, some delicious image had been enshrined in my heart, last thought at night, first thought in the morning. Fred Terry as Sir Percy Blakeney,

Lord Byron, Rudolph Valentino, Henry V, Gerald du Maurier, blissful Mrs Ashton at my school, Steerforth, Napoleon, the guard on the 4.45, image had succeeded image. Latterly it had been that of a pale pompous young man in the Foreign Office who had once, during my season in London, asked me for a dance, had seemed to me the very flower of cosmopolitan civilization, and had remained the pivot of existence until wiped from my memory by Sauveterre. For that is what always happened to these images. Time and hateful absence blurred them, faded them but never quite obliterated them until some lovely new broom image came and swept them away.

'There you are you see,' Mrs Chaddesley Corbett turned triumphantly to Lady Montdore. 'From kiddie-car to hearse, darling, I couldn't know it better. After all, what would there be to think about when one's alone, otherwise?'

from *Love in a Cold Climate*, Nancy Mitford

*The fact that she didn't speak to me once in two years did nothing to diminish my passion for my school prefect. Day and night I dreamed of rescuing her from fire and flood, but at thirteen with a guilty thrill of infidelity, I switched, like Nancy Mitford's Fanny, to men. In quick succession, Budge Patty, Richard Todd, Brian Close, Louis MacNeice, John Carol Case became the objects of my undying affection. Their photographs, cracked with kissing and being dragged about in my satchel, lay successively under my pillow. Often I cried myself to sleep at the sheer impossibility of any of them loving me back – but if Budge Patty or any of the others had descended from Olympus and tried to grab me behind the squash courts I should have died of horror. Like Tennyson's dog, I only hunted in dreams.*

*An awful lot of time at school seemed to be spent in church. Not being of a religious bent, this left me long hours to daydream, and gaze surreptitiously at the congregation and the more handsome members of the clergy. Sunshine streaming through a stained-glass window can throw a most becoming light on the golden head of a curate or a chorister. We were all madly in love with the Bishop of Sarum, of course, but there was nothing he could do about us. As Sydney Smith has pointed out:*

'How can a bishop marry? How can he flirt? The most he can say is, "I'll see you in the vestry after service".'

*I always feel John Betjeman must have dreamed up his poem,* Lenten Thoughts of a High Anglican, *during a boring sermon.*

Isn't she lovely, 'the Mistress'?
    With her wide-apart grey-green eyes,
The droop of her lips and, when she smiles,
    Her glance of amused surprise?

How nonchalantly she wears her clothes,
    How expensive they are as well!
And the sound of her voice is as soft and deep
    As the Christ Church tenor bell.

But why do I call her 'the Mistress'
    Who know not her way of life?
Because she has more of a cared-for air
    Than many a legal wife.

How elegantly she swings along
    In the vapoury incense veil;
The angel choir must pause in song
    When she kneels at the altar rail.

The parson said that we shouldn't stare
    Around when we come to church,
Or the Unknown God we are seeking
    May forever elude our search.

But I hope the preacher will not think
    It unorthodox and odd
If I add that I glimpse in 'the Mistress'
    A hint of the Unknown God.

♥
♥ ♥
♥

# Getting Off The Mark

*The British are very slow at getting off the mark with the opposite sex. The working classes solve the problem by hunting in pairs, as Keith Waterhouse points out in The Duck Walk. The upper class young, according to Douglas Sutherland, can't afford tarts any more so they resort to bread rolls.*

The polling station was a local school. Straggling past the school, as I went in, were two pairs of teenaged girls and two pairs of teenaged boys.

Each pair independent of the others. Walking, according to sex, in opposite directions.

Coming out of the school, I was surprised to see the same two pairs of teenaged girls and the same two pairs of teenaged boys.

Still walking in opposite directions. But this time, if you follow me, in OPPOSITE opposite directions.

Clearly, they'd all been to their respective ends of the street, then retraced their steps. But why? They weren't taking a constitutional, because teenagers don't take constitutionals. They weren't waiting for their mums, because they would have regarded themselves as above the mum-waiting age. They weren't demonstrating for votes at fifteen, because they didn't have placards. So what were they up to?

Then, as the first pair of girls passed the second pair of boys, I saw two sets of female shoulders shaking in a repressed fit of the giggles. And the penny dropped. What I'd stumbled across was the local duck-walk.

If you do not know what a duck-walk is, have no fear. I am about to tell you more about the subject than you can possibly need to know.

A duck-walk is a length of pavement, stretch of recreation ground, boating-lake perimeter, park-bandstand circumference, shopping-parade diameter, or any other form of measured mile give or take a hundred yards or so, where the lads and lasses of the town perambulate in the hope of – to use the phrase of my own long-lost youth – getting off with each other.

I didn't know the institution still existed. I thought it all happened in youth clubs and discotheques these days.

For the record, the two pairs of teenaged boys outside my polling station successfully got off with the two pairs of teenaged girls. But I'm afraid I can't report to you on the technique employed. I was already back in my world of boogie-woogie, Arthur English ties, milk-shakes, Andy Hardy films – and the duck-walk.

There were several duck-walks where I used to live. One in the park, one around the parish church, one in the middle of the bluebell woods for advanced practitioners, and one near the public library. The public library concession was the one most favoured by my best friend and me.

Duck-walk etiquette required that you had to have your best friend with you – one of you brilliantined to the eyebrows, the other not. In the case of the girls, the rule seemed to be that the one most closely approximating Doris Day should be accompanied by a juvenile Martha Raye, or an old boot as she was colloquially known.

I believe the process is called natural selection.

The main advantage of the duck-walk was that you were able to examine the goods at leisure before you bought them. If you and your best friend didn't fancy Doris Day and Martha Raye, it was like the conductress always used to say when the last tram was full: 'There'll be another along in a minute.'

You strolled, always in pairs, from north to south or south to north depending on your sex; or, in the case of the boating-lake, clockwise or anti-clockwise; or, in the case of the advanced practitioners in the bluebell woods, a zig-zag course ending in screams of terror (I think they were screams of terror) among the deep ferns.

As for the public library route, the drill was this. Say you're my best friend and I'm me, and Doris Day and Martha Raye are walking down from the chip-shop limits of the duck-walk. Just as they're minneying by with their noses stuck in the air, we make a clicking noise with our tongues, which naturally enough they ignore.

But we watch them very carefully when they've gone by. If one of them gives the other a shove fit to send her into the gutter, it means we've made it. In the vernacular, we've clicked.

On with the ritual. They get as far as the public library and retrace their steps. We reach the chip-shop and retrace ours. Thus we meet again, this being a small world. And after a bit of badinage, such as, 'Does your mother know you're out?' or, 'Are there any more at home like you?' to which the witty response might be, 'Get off your knees!' or, 'Go on home, your mother wants your boots for loaf tins,' a lifelong friendship lasting at least two weeks is struck up.

Guess who gets Doris Day. And guess who gets the old boot.

Still, they were happy days. And are still, apparently. And I didn't talk about the election, did I?

*The Duck Walk*, Keith Waterhouse

This is not to say that a young gentleman's education in matters of sex is entirely neglected. His mother may mutter on about the birds and the bees but who wants to listen to all that rot when he can watch his pet guinea pigs in action any day of the week? It is just that he cannot quite visualize himself doing the same thing and he secretly rather hopes that babies really are born under gooseberry bushes.

The result is that most young gentlemen start out in life regarding all females with considerable suspicion.

Inevitably there comes the time when the young ladies and gentlemen are forced into each others' arms at those strange upper-class fertility rites known as debutante dances and it is hard to say which sex is the more embarrassed. The boys assert their manhood by throwing bread rolls, drinking too much champagne and being sick in the bushes while the girls defy their anxious and ambitious parents by running off with any unsuitable bounder who has somehow managed to gatecrash the party.

In more spacious days indulgent fathers used to have their sons instructed in the facts of life by introducing them to one of the many houses in London run by Madams who, so legend went, had hearts of gold. Nowadays, however, professional ladies find it more lucrative and less exhausting to devote themselves to comforting out-of-town businessmen, and young gentlemen find themselves relegated to the amateur league which operates around the coffee bars of the King's Road, Chelsea. The enthusiastic free-for-all which has resulted has made London the envy of her continental neighbours.

from *The English Gentleman*, Douglas Sutherland

*'Of all forms of caution,' wrote Bertrand Russell, 'caution in love is perhaps the most fatal to true happiness.' When we are young we are often far too shy to capitalize on a situation. We plot, we dream, then when the ideal moment comes, we funk it, as the boy in Thomas Hardy's poem found to his cost:*

> She wore a new 'terra-cotta' dress,
> And we stayed, because of the pelting storm,
> Within the hansom's dry recess,
> Though the horse had stopped; yea, motionless
>     We sat on, snug and warm.
>
> Then the downpour ceased, to my sharp sad pain,
> And the glass that had screened our forms before
> Flew up, and out she sprang to her door:
> I should have kissed her if the rain
>     Had lasted a minute more.

A *Thunderstorm in Town*, Thomas Hardy

*It is mostly when we are young that love strikes like a thunder-bolt – the* coup de foudre *the French call it – so that every-*

*thing else is put aside. Marlowe thought this was the only way true love could develop. Juliet, on the other hand, even at the age of fourteen, liked a relationship to develop more slowly:*

> It lies not in our power to love, or hate,
> For will in us is over-rul'd by fate.
> When two are stripped, long ere the course begin,
> We wish that one should lose, the other win;
> And one especially do we affect
> Of two gold ingots, like in each respect.
> The reason no man knows; let it suffice
> What we behold is censured by our eyes.
> Where both deliberate, the love is slight;
> Who ever loved that loved not at first sight?

from *Hero and Leander*, Christopher Marlowe

> It is too rash, too unadvis'd, too sudden;
> Too like the lightning, which doth cease to be
> Ere one can say it lightens. Sweet, good-night!
> This bud of love, by summer's ripening breath,
> May prove a beauteous flower when next we meet.

from *Romeo and Juliet*, William Shakespeare

*Another tragic victim of the* coup de foudre *was the Lady of Shalott, who sat weaving away in her tower, accepting her captivity with equanimity, until suddenly Sir Lancelot came riding by. Next moment she had left the loom, and her terrible fate was sealed.*

*This is one of the great ironic love stories because when the Lady of Shalott dies in the end, and all the knights and townspeople are crossing themselves with fear, Lancelot, totally unaware that he has been the cause of her destruction, is alone struck by her beauty and blesses her:*

> There she weaves by night and day
> A magic web with colours gay.
> She has heard a whisper say,

A curse is on her if she stay
   To look down to Camelot.
She knows not what the curse may be,
And so she weaveth steadily,
And little other care hath she,
   The Lady of Shalott.

And moving thro' a mirror clear
That hangs before her all the year,
Shadows of the world appear.
There she sees the highway near
   Winding down to Camelot:
There the river eddy whirls,
And there the surly village-churls,
And the red cloaks of market girls,
   Pass onward from Shalott.

Sometimes a troop of damsels glad,
An abbot on an ambling pad,
Sometimes a curly shepherd-lad,
Or long-hair'd page in crimson clad,
   Goes by to tower'd Camelot;
And sometimes thro' the mirror blue
The knights come riding two and two:
She hath no loyal knight and true,
   The Lady of Shalott.

But in her web she still delights
To weave the mirror's magic sights,
For often thro' the silent nights
A funeral, with plumes and lights,
   And music, went to Camelot:
Or when the moon was overhead,
Came two young lovers lately wed;
'I am half sick of shadows,' said
   The Lady of Shalott.

A bow-shot from her bower-eaves,
He rode between the barley-sheaves,

The sun came dazzling thro' the leaves,
And flamed upon the brazen greaves
   Of bold Sir Lancelot.
A red-cross knight for ever kneel'd
To a lady in his shield,
That sparkled on the yellow field,
   Beside remote Shalott.

The gemmy bridle glitter'd free,
Like to some branch of stars we see
Hung in the golden Galaxy,
The bridle bells rang merrily
   As he rode down to Camelot:
And from his blazon'd baldric slung
A mighty silver bugle hung,
And as he rode his armour rung,
   Beside remote Shalott.

All in the blue unclouded weather
Thick-jewell'd shone the saddle-leather,
The helmet and the helmet-feather
Burn'd like one burning flame together,
   As he rode down to Camelot.
As often thro' the purple night,
Below the starry clusters bright,
Some bearded meteor, trailing light,
   Moves over still Shalott.

His broad clear brow in sunlight glow'd;
On burnish'd hooves his war-horse trode;
From underneath his helmet flow'd
His coal-black curls as on he rode,
   As he rode down to Camelot.
From the bank and from the river
He flash'd into the crystal mirror,
'Tirra lirra,' by the river
   Sang Sir Lancelot.

She left the web, she left the loom,
She made three paces thro' the room,
She saw the water-lily bloom,
She saw the helmet and the plume,
   She look'd down to Camelot.
Out flew the web and floated wide;
The mirror crack'd from side to side;
'The curse is come upon me!' cried
   The Lady of Shalott.

In the stormy east-wind straining,
The pale yellow woods were waning,
The broad stream in his banks complaining,
Heavily the low sky raining
   Over tower'd Camelot;
Down she came and found a boat
Beneath a willow left afloat,
And round about the prow she wrote
   *The Lady of Shalott.*

And down the river's dim expanse
Like some bold seer in a trance,
Seeing all his own mischance –
With a glassy countenance
   Did she look to Camelot.
And at the closing of the day
She loosed the chain, and down she lay;
The broad stream bore her far away,
   The Lady of Shalott.

Lying, robed in snowy white
That loosely flew to left and right –
The leaves upon her falling light –
Thro' the noises of the night
   She floated down to Camelot:
And as the boat-head wound along
The willowy hills and fields among,
They heard her singing her last song,
   The Lady of Shalott.

Heard a carol, mournful, holy,
Chanted loudly, chanted lowly,
Till her blood was frozen slowly,
And her eyes were darken'd wholly,
    Turn'd to tower'd Camelot;
For ere she reach'd upon the tide
The first house by the water-side,
Singing in her song she died,
    The Lady of Shalott.

Under tower and balcony,
By garden-wall and gallery,
A gleaming shape she floated by,
Dead-pale between the houses high,
    Silent into Camelot.
Out upon the wharfs they came,
Knight and burgher, lord and dame,
And round the prow they read her name,
    *The Lady of Shalott.*

Who is this? and what is here?
And in the lighted palace near
Died the sound of royal cheer;
And they cross'd themselves for fear,
    All the knights at Camelot:
But Lancelot mused a little space;
He said, 'She has a lovely face;
God in His mercy lend her grace,
    The Lady of Shalott'.

from *The Lady of Shalott,*
Alfred, Lord Tennyson

The Lady of Shalott *is a poem which I adored as a child. I think the brilliant colours appealed to me: the red cloaks of the market girls, the crimson of the page, the blue unclouded weather, the purple night, the flowing coal-black curls of Sir Lancelot, the pale yellow woods, and finally the ghostly white dress of the Lady of Shalott. One is also dazzled by the arrival* of Sir Lancelot. The Lady has just confessed she is sick of shadows, and suddenly he swans in all fire and glitter and care-free vitality, with the sun glinting on his shield, his plumed helmet, his gemmy bridle and thickly jewelled saddle, bells ringing, armour jangling, singing as he goes.

No doubt schoolgirls today giggle at the line about 'Sir Lancelot flashing into the crystal mirror', just as in our day we giggled about the Lady of Shalott complaining that the curse had come upon her.

'No wonder the poor thing looked deathly pale and had to have a lie down in the boat,' I remember my best friend saying.

One notices, too, the skilful way Tennyson used the weather to denote a change of mood. As Sir Lancelot arrives, the sun comes dazzling through the leaves, the sky is cloudless, but the moment the Lady of Shalott leaves the room the temperature drops, a stormy east wind gets up, the colour drains out of the woods and the rain begins.

One is reminded of Shakespeare's lovely lines from Two Gentlemen of Verona:

> O! how this spring of love resembleth
> The uncertain glory of an April Day
> Which now shows all the beauty of the sun,
> And by and by a cloud takes all away!

# No Accounting For Tastes

Sir Lancelot's attractions were obvious enough to make the Lady of Shalott exchange the loom for her doom. But people are often puzzled why one person is drawn to another. What does he see in her? they ask. Probably no more initially than a favourable reflection of himself in the girl's eyes. Some men, on the other hand, fancy the Princess Lointaine: 'She whom I love is hard to catch and conquer,' wrote Meredith,

Hard, but O the glory of the winning were she won!

Auden, for example, wrote a poem about a brilliant man who appeared to have everything, money, fame, masses of friends, but who was eating his heart out for rather an ordinary girl who didn't return his affection:

A shilling life will give you all the facts:
How Father beat him, how he ran away,
What were the struggles of his youth, what acts
Made him the greatest figure of his day:
Of how he fought, fished, hunted, worked all night,
Though giddy, climbed new mountains; named a sea:
Some of the last researchers even write
Love made him weep pints like you and me.

With all his honours on, he sighed for one
Who, say astonished critics, lived at home;
Did little jobs about the house with skill
And nothing else; could whistle; would sit still
Or potter round the garden; answered some
Of his long marvellous letters but kept none.

*Who's Who*, W. H. Auden

*The secret of this person's charm was obviously her unavailability. If she'd turned round and said, 'Give me a sapphire flanked with diamonds and let's pop down to John Lewis and look at curtain material,' he'd have probably run a mile. Although it must be pointed out that in Auden's case the poem was written to a boy.*

*John Betjeman is attracted to chaste, capable Amazons:*

> Pam, I adore you, Pam, you great big mountainous sports
> girl,
> Whizzing them over the net, full of the strength of five:
> That old Malvernian brother, you zephyr and khaki shorts
> girl,
> Although he's playing for Woking,
> Can't stand up
> To your wonderful backhand drive.

> from *Pot Pourri From A Surrey Garden*, John Betjeman

*The British, too, are notoriously class-conscious. One remembers Mr Darcy fighting manfully to dispel his passion for Elizabeth Bennet, because he thought she was so far beneath him in station and her relations were so frightful. Both Tennyson and Betjeman, on the other hand, seem immune to the charms of the aristocratic woman:*

> At me you smiled, but unbeguiled
> I saw the snare and I retired;
> The daughter of a hundred Earls,
> You are not one to be desired.

> *Lady Clara Vere de Vere*,
> Alfred, Lord Tennyson

> Keep me from Thelma's sister Pearl!
> She puts my senses in a whirl,
> Weakens my knees and keeps me waiting
> Until my heart stops palpitating.

The debs may turn disdainful backs
On Pearl's uncouth mechanic slacks,
And outraged see the fire that lies
And smoulders in her long-lashed eyes.

Have they such weather-freckled features,
The smooth sophisticated creatures?
Ah, not to them such limbs belong,
Such animal movements sure and strong.

Such arms to take a man and press
In agricultural caress
His head to hers, and hold him there
Deep buried in her chestnut hair.

God shrive me from this morning lust
For supple farm girls: if you must,
Send the cold daughter of an earl –
But spare me Thelma's sister Pearl!

*Agricultural Caress*, John Betjeman

*Gilbert on the other hand put in a plea for the upper classes:*

Spurn not the nobly born With love affected,
Nor treat with virtuous scorn The well-connected.
Hearts just as pure and fair
May beat in Belgrave Square,
As in the lowly air
  Of Seven Dials.

*Iolanthe*, W. S. Gilbert

*Women often believe they make themselves attractive by spending hours on their appearance. One remembers the famous passage in* Forever Amber, *when Amber actually spent three days dressing for a ball in order to win back a lover. It didn't work. He stayed with his new wife, who was much quieter, and who bothered much less with her looks. Ben Jonson and Herrick also preferred girls who dressed casually:*

Give me a look, give me a face,
That makes simplicity a grace;
Robes loosely flowing, hair as free:
Such sweet neglect more taketh me,
Than all the adulteries of art;
They strike mine eyes, but not my heart.

*Epicoene*, Ben Jonson

A sweet disorder in the dress
Kindles in clothes a wantonness:
A lawn about the shoulders thrown
Into a fine distraction:
An erring lace, which here and there,
Enthrals the crimson stomacher:
A cuff neglectful, and thereby
Ribbands to flow confusedly:
A winning wave (deserving note)
In the tempestuous petticoat:
A careless shoe-string, in whose tie
I see a wild civility:
Do more bewitch me, than when Art
Is too precise in every part!

*Delight in Disorder*, Robert Herrick

*Different shapes also attract different men. Edmund Waller
was turned on by a slender waist. Tennyson's married man
adored Maud because she was tall and stately, and Byron
vowed he hated a dumpy woman. A friend of my father, however, once said his favourite things in life were hot baths, duck
and green peas, and fat jolly girls, in that order. And Sydney
Smith knew a man who preferred his women positively gar-
gantuan: a young Scot who was about to marry an Irish widow,
twice his age and more than twice his size.*

'Going to marry her!' cried Sydney Smith, 'going to marry her!
Impossible! You mean a part of her; he could not marry her

all himself. It would be a case, not of bigamy, but trigamy; the neighbourhood or the magistrates should interfere. There is enough of her to furnish wives for a whole parish. One man marry her! It is monstrous! You might people a colony with her; or give an assembly with her; or perhaps take your morning's walk round her, always provided there are frequent resting-places, and you were in rude health. I once was rash enough to try walking round her before breakfast, but only got half-way and gave it up exhausted. Or you might read the Riot Act and disperse her; in short, you might do anything with her but marry her.'

## Obsession

The trouble with being in love is that you can't concentrate on anything else. How well I remember sitting in an office snivelling into a Kleenex playing 'He loves me, he loves me not' with raindrops down the window, incapable of even typing 'Dear Sir', because the only Sir who was dear to me hadn't rung up for a couple of days. Only a woman, I think, can appreciate the nightmare of being dependent on the telephone:

> Full of desire I lay, the sky wounding me,
> each cloud a ship without me sailing, each tree
> possessing what my soul lacked, tranquillity.
>
> Waiting for the longed-for voice to speak
> through the mute telephone, my body grew weak
> with the well-known and mortal death, heartbreak.
>
> from *Passion*, Kathleen Raine

*Robert Graves and Congreve both saw this obsessive love as a sickness:*

I am melancholy when thou art absent; look like an ass when thou art present; wake for thee, when I should sleep, and even dream of thee, when I am awake; sigh much, drink little, eat less, court solitude, am grown very entertaining to my self, and (as I am informed) very troublesome to everybody else. If this be not love, it is madness and then it is pardonable.

> from *The Old Bachelor*, William Congreve

> Love is a universal migraine,
> A bright stain on the vision
> Blotting out reason.

Symptoms of true love
Are leanness, jealousy
Laggard dawns;

Are omens and nightmares —
Listening for a knock,
Waiting for a sign:

For a touch of her fingers
In a darkened room,
For a searching look.

Take courage, lover!
Can you endure such grief,
At any hand but hers?

*Symptoms of Love,*
Robert Graves

*Love, said Goldsmith, is an abject intercourse between tyrant and slave. Shakespeare seems to agree with him. When I was taking a secretarial course at Oxford, one of the first exercises we were set was to type the following sonnet without a mistake. I was hopelessly in love at the time with a handsome Czechoslovakian undergraduate who was reading Engineering. He was one of those naturally attractive men who charmed anything he met, even if it were only a cat sunning itself on a red brick wall in the Banbury Road. I managed to type the sonnet perfectly each time until I reached the lines:*

But, like a sad slave, stay and think of nought
Save, where you are, how happy you make those.

Being your slave, what should I do but tend
Upon the hours and times of your desire?
I have no precious time at all to spend,
Nor services to do, till you require.
Nor dare I chide the world-without-end hour
Whilst I, my sovereign, watch the clock for you,
Nor think the bitterness of absence sour;

When you have bid your servant once adieu;
Nor dare I question with my jealous thought
Where you may be, or your affairs suppose,
But, like a sad slave, stay and think of nought
Save, where you are, how happy you make those.
　So true a fool is love that in your will,
　Though you do anything, he thinks no ill.

*Sonnet LVII*, William Shakespeare

*Now to three poems with which I used to identify when I was
in this hopelessly obsessed, unrequited state:*

Follow thy fair sun, unhappy shadow,
　Though thou be black as night,
　And she made all of light,
Yet follow thy fair sun, unhappy shadow.

from *A Book of Airs*,
Thomas Campion

It is not that I love you less
Than when before your feet I lay:
But to prevent the sad increase
Of hopeless love, I keep away.

In vain (alas) for everything
Which I have knowne belong to you,
Your Forme does to my Fancy bring,
And makes my old wounds bleed anew.

Who in the Spring from the new Sun,
Already had a Fever got,
Too late begins these shafts to shun,
Which Phoebus through his veines has shot,

Too late he would the pains assuage,
And to thick shadows does retire;
About with him he beares the rage,
And in his tainted blood the Fire.

But vow'd I have, and never must
Your banish'd servant trouble you;
For if I breake, you may mistrust
The vow I made to love you too.

*The Selfe Banished*, Edmund Waller

They flee from me that sometime did me seek,
   With naked foot stalking within my chamber:
Once have I seen them gentle, tame, and meek,
   That now are wild, and do not once remember
   That sometime they have put themselves in danger
To take bread at my hand; and now they range
Busily seeking in continual change.

Thanked be fortune, it hath been otherwise
   Twenty times better; but once especial
In thin array: after a pleasant guise,
   When her loose gown did from her shoulders fall,
   And she me caught in her arms long and small,
And therewithal so sweetly did me kiss,
And softly said, 'Dear heart, how like you this?'

It was no dream; for I lay broad awaking:
   But all is turn'd now through my gentleness
Into a bitter fashion of forsaking;
   And I have leave to go of her goodness;
   And she also to use new-fangleness.
But since that I unkindly so am servèd,
'How like you this?' – what hath she now deservèd?

*Remembrance*, Thomas Wyatt

*I was particularly haunted by Wyatt's lines:*

But all is turn'd now through my gentleness
Into a bitter fashion of forsaking

*because they seemed to capture all the horror of having some-
one cooling off you. They reminded me of that sad, sad line in
King Lear:*

> I have observed a faint neglect of late.

*A plea for love to continue is another gambit of the lover. Let
us be faithful, he cries, because our love is the only thing we
can cling on to in a frightening and impermanent world.
Matthew Arnold and Dante Gabriel Rossetti both wrote well
on this subject:*

> Ah, love, let us be true
> To one another! for the world, which seems
> To lie before us like a land of dreams,
> So various, so beautiful, so new,
> Hath really neither joy, nor love, nor light,
> Nor certitude, nor peace, nor help for pain;
> And we are here as on a darkling plain
> Swept with confused alarms of struggle and flight,
> Where ignorant armies clash by night.

> from *Dover Beach*, Matthew Arnold

> When do I see thee most, beloved one?
>     When in the light the spirits of mine eyes
>     Before thy face, their altar, solemnize
> The worship of that Love through thee made known?
> Or when in the dusk hours, (we two alone,)
>     Close-kissed and eloquent of still replies
>     Thy twilight-hidden glimmering visage lies,
> And my soul only sees thy soul its own?
> O love, my love! if I no more should see
> Thyself, nor on the earth the shadow of thee,
>     Nor image of thine eyes in any spring, –
> How then should sound upon Life's darkening slope
> The ground-whirl of the perished leaves of Hope,
>     The wind of Death's imperishable wing?

> *Lovesight*, Dante Gabriel Rossetti

*Rochester, the great Restoration rake, however, argues that it is only possible to live and love in the present:*

> All my past Life is mine no more,
>     The flying Hours are gone:
> Like transitory Dreams giv'n o'er,
> Whose Images are kept in store
>     By Memory alone.
>
> The Time that is to come is not;
>     How can it then be mine?
> The present Moment's all my Lot;
> And that, as fast as it is got,
>     Phillis, is only thine.
>
> Then talk not of Inconstancy,
>     False Hearts, and broken Vows;
> If I by Miracle can be
> This live-long Minute true to thee,
>     'Tis all that Heav'n allows.
>
> *Love and Life. A Song,*
> John Wilmot, Earl of Rochester

*Another argument that never holds much water with the loved one is that you may not have much to offer except the distinction of loving them far more than anyone else.*

*'I know I can make you happy, Jill,' the occasional, frightful, sweaty-faced stockbroker used to say, gazing fervently into my eyes. I knew perfectly well he couldn't, and always had to repress a terrible urge to cross my eyes and squint back at him. How callously indifferent to his suffering I was. Perhaps if he'd been able to write as well as Swinburne I might have felt differently:*

> Sweet, does death hurt? thou canst not do me wrong:
> I shall not lack thee, as I loved thee, long.
> Hast thou not given me above all that live
> Joy, and a little sorrow shalt not give?

What even though fairer fingers of strange girls
Pass nestling through thy beautiful boy's curls
As mine did, or those curled lithe lips of thine
Meet theirs as these, all theirs come after mine;
And though I were not, though I be not, best,
I have loved and love thee more than all the rest.

I shall remember while the light lives yet,
And in the night-time I shall not forget.
Though (as thou wilt) thou leave me ere life leave,
I will not, for thy love I will not grieve;
Not as they use who love not more than I,
Who love not as I love thee though I die;
And though thy lips, once mine, be oftener prest
To many another brow and balmier breast,
And sweeter arms, or sweeter to thy mind,
Lull thee or lure, more fond thou wilt not find.

from *Erotion*, Algernon Charles Swinburne

*Hilaire Belloc is not someone with whom one associates love poetry, but he wrote two brief, perfect verses. The first describes our total indifference to our surroundings when we are obsessed with someone else. The second, even more poignant, shows how we try to kid ourselves everything is all right, even when a love affair is going wrong:*

How did the party go in Portman Square?
I cannot tell you; Juliet was not there.
And how did Lady Gaster's party go?
Juliet was next me and I do not know.

*Juliet*, Hilaire Belloc

I said to Heart, 'How goes it?' Heart replied:
'Right as a Ribstone Pippin!' But it lied.

*The False Heart*, Hilaire Belloc

*Shakespeare tried to harbour the same tragic self-delusions when he began one of his last sonnets with the words:*

> When my love swears that she is made of truth,
> I do believe her, though I know she lies.

*'Many a tear has to fall,' goes the pop song, 'but it's all in the game.' 'Love's feeling,' said Shakespeare, 'is more soft and sensible than are the tender horns of cockled snails.' For this reason, when we're terribly in love, we often think things are over when they're perfectly all right. Dryden shows what bliss it is to make up after such doubts:*

> After the pangs of a desperate Lover,
> When day and night I have sigh'd all in vain,
> Ah what a pleasure it is to discover
> In her eyes pity, who causes my pain!
>
> When with unkindness our love at a stand is,
> And both have punish'd our selves with the pain,
> Ah what a pleasure the touch of her hand is,
> Ah what a pleasure to press it again!
>
> When the denyal comes fainter and fainter,
> And her eyes give what her tongue does deny,
> Ah what a trembling I feel when I venture,
> Ah what a trembling does usher my joy!
>
> When, with a Sigh, she accords me the blessing,
> And her eyes twinkle 'twixt pleasure and pain;
> Ah what a joy 'tis beyond all expressing,
> Ah what a joy to hear, shall we again!

from *An Evening's Love*, John Dryden

## Love Letters

One way of relieving the heart-ache is to write love letters –
pouring one's heart out with the aid of The Oxford Dictionary
of Quotations. 'You write marvellous letters, Jill,' I remember
one barrister saying to me, 'but they are rather hard to
answer.' Here is a letter from Dorothy Osborne to her lover,
Sir William Temple, written just after the Civil War. William
was on the King's side, which made it impossible for them to
marry for some years. Here we see Dorothy fretting at the
enforced separation.

Last night I was in the garden until eleven o'clock. It was the
sweetest night that e'er I saw. The garden looked so well and
the jessamine smelt beyond all perfume. And yet I was not
pleased. The place had all the charms it used to have when I
was most satisfied with it, and had you been there I should
have liked it much more than ever I did; but that not being, it
was no more to me than the next field . . .

Later Dorothy caught smallpox which destroyed her beauty.
But so great was Sir William's love that he still wanted to
marry her – and they had a long and happy life together.
  Now a letter from Keats to his girlfriend Fanny Brawne.
Although the writing is slightly self-conscious, and probably
aimed at posterity as much as the loved one, the suffering is
no less real.

My love has made me selfish. I cannot exist without you. I am
forgetful of everything but seeing you again – my life seems to
stop there – I see no further. You have absorb'd me. I have a
sensation at the present moment as though I was dissolving –

I should be exquisitely miserable without the hope of soon seeing you. My sweet Fanny, will your heart never change? My love, will it? I have no limit now to my love ... Your note came – it is just here. I cannot be happier away from you. 'Tis richer than an argosy of Pearles. Do not thwart me even in jest. I have been astonished that men could die Martyrs for religion – I have shuddered at it. I shudder no more – I could be martyr'd for my Religion – Love is my religion. I could die for that. I could die for you.

*Letter to Fanny Brawne*, John Keats

*We end with two letters from Oscar Wilde. The first, written in 1884, is the only letter to his wife Constance which is known to have survived. The rest were almost certainly destroyed by her, or by her family. The second letter, written in 1893, is to Lord Alfred Douglas. The passion in both letters is tragically ironic but if I had been Constance Wilde I am not sure if I would have liked the line about her bodily presence there not being able to make her more real.*

Tuesday [*Postmark 16 December 1884*]          The Balmoral,
                                                Edinburgh

Dear and Beloved, Here am I, and you at the Antipodes. O execrable facts, that keep our lips from kissing, though our souls are one.

What can I tell you by letter? Alas! nothing that I would tell you. The messages of the gods to each other travel not by pen and ink and indeed your bodily presence here would not make you more real: for I feel your fingers in my hair, and your cheek brushing mine. The air is full of the music of your voice, my soul and body seem no longer mine, but mingled in some exquisite ecstasy with yours. I feel incomplete without you.

Ever and ever yours                                     Oscar
Here I stay till Sunday.

[? *January 1893*] [*Babbacombe Cliff*]

My Own Boy, Your sonnet is quite lovely, and it is a marvel that those red rose-leaf lips of yours should have been made no less for music of song than for madness of kisses. Your slim gilt soul walks between passion and poetry. I know Hyacinthus, whom Apollo loved so madly, was you in Greek days.

Why are you alone in London, and when do you go to Salisbury? Do go there to cool your hands in the grey twilight of Gothic things, and come here whenever you like. It is a lovely place — it only lacks you; but go to Salisbury first. Always, with undying love, yours

Oscar

# Coming On Too Strong
## and How To Control It

The maddening thing about love is that one can never synchronize one's watches. 'The fickleness of the women I love,' said Shaw, 'is only equalled by the infernal constancy of the women who love me.' 'Please make Tom, Dick or Harry fall in love with me,' I used to pray to the new moon, 'but not too much or he'll get all soppy and I'll go off him.' How often have I rolled up, dripping Arpège, tongue hanging out, for a lecherous lunch with a glamorous man, only to discover that he's decided to go back to his girlfriend and wants my advice on the best way to go about it? But if one is of a romantic disposition it's almost impossible to keep one's feelings in check. Yeats, Housman and Auden have all written moving poems on this subject:

Down by the salley gardens my love and I did meet;
She passed the salley gardens with little snow-white feet.
She bid me take love easy, as the leaves grow on the tree;
But I, being young and foolish, with her would not agree.

In a field by the river my love and I did stand,
And on my leaning shoulder she laid her snow-white hand.
She bid me take life easy, as the grass grows on the weirs;
But I was young and foolish, and now am full of tears.

*Down by the Salley Gardens*, W. B. Yeats

When I was one-and-twenty
    I heard a wise man say,
'Give crowns and pounds and guineas
    But not your heart away;

Give pearls away and rubies
    But keep your fancy free.'
But I was one-and-twenty,
    No use to talk to me.

When I was one-and-twenty
    I heard him say again,
'The heart out of the bosom
    Was never given in vain;
'Tis paid with sighs a plenty
    And sold for endless rue.'
And I am two-and-twenty,
    And oh, 'tis true, 'tis true.

                  A. E. Housman

Oh the valley in the summer when I and my John
Beside the deep river would walk on and on
While the flowers at our feet and the birds up above
Argued so sweetly on reciprocal love,
And I leaned on his shoulder; 'O Johnny, let's play':
But he frowned like thunder and he went away.

O that Friday near Christmas as I well recall
When we went to the Charity Matinée Ball,
The floor was so smooth and the band was so loud
And Johnny so handsome I felt so proud;
'Squeeze me tighter, dear Johnny, let's dance till it's day':
But he frowned like thunder and he went away.

Shall I ever forget at the Grand Opera
When music poured out of each wonderful star?
Diamonds and pearls they hung dazzling down
Over each silver or golden silk gown;
'Oh John I'm in Heaven', I whispered to say:
But he frowned like thunder and he went away.

O but he was fair as a garden in flower,
As slender and tall as the great Eiffel Tower
When the waltz throbbed out on the long promenade

O his eyes and his smile they went straight to my heart;
'O marry me, Johnny, I'll love and obey':
But he frowned like thunder and he went away.

from *Johnny*, W. H. Auden

*It is terribly easy to advise other people who are unhappy in love. Poets have been doing it for years. Yeats believed in playing it cool. Sir John Suckling thought it was very bad technique, mooning around looking sick with love. Cleopatra believed in keeping her lovers guessing, and crossing them in everything. Nat Gubbins believed it was better policy to cross them in nothing.*

Never give all the heart, for love
Will hardly seem worth thinking of
To passionate women if it seem
Certain, and they never dream
That it fades out from kiss to kiss;
For everything that's lovely is
But a brief dreamy kind delight.
O never give the heart outright,
For they, for all smooth lips can say,
Have given their hearts up to the play.
And who could play it well enough
If deaf and dumb and blind with love?
He that made this knows all the cost
For he gave all his heart and lost.

*Never Give All the Heart*,
W. B. Yeats

Why so pale and wan, fond lover?
        Prithee, why so pale?
Will, when looking well can't move her,
        Looking ill prevail?
        Prithee, why so pale?

Why so dull and mute, young sinner?
    Prithee why so mute?
Will, when speaking well can't win her,
    Saying nothing do't?
    Prithee, why so mute?

Quit, quit for shame! This will not move;
    This cannot take her;
If of herself she will not love,
    Nothing can make her:
    The devil take her!

*Why So Pale and Wan,*
Sir John Suckling

*(Cleopatra is talking to one of her ladies in waiting, Charmian, about Antony)*

*Cleopatra:* Where is he?
*Charmian:* I did not see him since.
*Cleopatra:* (To the messenger Alexas) See where he is, who's with him, what he does:
  I did not send you: If you find him sad,
  Say I am dancing; if in mirth, report
  That I am sudden sick: quick and return.
    *Exit Alexas*
*Charmian:* Madam, methinks, if you did love him dearly,
  You do not hold the method to enforce
  The like from him.
*Cleopatra:* What should I do I do not?
*Charmian:* In each thing give him way, cross him in nothing.
*Cleopatra:* Thou teachest like a fool; the way to lose him.

from *Antony and Cleopatra*, William Shakespeare

MRS MIFFINS ON "OW TO GIT YORE MAN'
The first thing to remember is to git interested in yore man's work.
If it's pigs git interested in pigs and if it's leaky taps and

cisterns like mr bumbling's git interested in leaky taps and cisterns.

As I 'ave said before most gentlemen prefer the larky sporty tipe, but there are also those wot prefers the quiet moony tipe so you will 'ave to be larky and sporty or quiet and moony accordin' to the man you are chasin'.

from the *Sunday Express*, Nathaniel Gubbins

# Courting With Poetry

*Poets through the ages have courted women with their verses. Some lovers, like Thomas Carew, were merely content to list their mistress's perfections, presenting a picture as idealistically beautiful and unreal as a Playboy nude. Shakespeare had no such illusions about his dark lady, but his appreciation of her charms was far more honest. One wonders though whether she was very flattered by such a description – dun breasts, wiry hair, indifferent breath – perhaps that's why she started giving him such a hard time.*

> Ask me no more where Jove bestows,
> When June is past, the fading rose;
> For in your beauty's orient deep
> These flowers, as in their causes, sleep.
>
> . . . .
>
> Ask me no more whither doth haste
> The nightingale when May is past;
> For in your sweet dividing throat
> She winters and keeps warm her note.
>
> . . . .
>
> Ask me no more if East or West
> The Phoenix builds her spicy nest;
> For unto you at last she flies,
> And in your fragrant bosom dies.
>
> from *Song*, Thomas Carew

My mistress' eyes are nothing like the sun;
Coral is far more red than her lips' red:
If snow be white, why then her breasts are dun;
If hairs be wires, black wires grow on her head.

I have seen roses damask'd, red and white,
But no such roses see I in her cheeks;
And in some perfumes is there more delight
Than in the breath that from my mistress reeks.
I love to hear her speak, yet well I know
That music has a far more pleasing sound:
I grant I never saw a goddess go, —
My mistress, when she walks, treads on the ground:
    And yet, by heaven, I think my love as rare
    As any she belied with false compare.

*Sonnet CXXX*, William Shakespeare

*Other poets employed the technique of praising a woman's beauty to the heights, then slyly pointing out that she'd better make the most of it, preferably giving them first refusal, as beauty doesn't last. Following this formula, Edmund Waller wrote one of the most beautiful poems in the English language:*

Go, lovely Rose —
Tell her that wastes her time and me
    That now she knows,
When I resemble her to thee,
How sweet and fair she seems to be.

    Tell her that's young,
And shuns to have her graces spied,
    That hadst thou sprung
In deserts where no men abide,
Thou must have uncommended died.

    Small is the worth
Of beauty from the light retired:
    Bid her come forth,
Suffer herself to be desired,
And not blush so to be admired.

Then die – that she
The common fate of all things rare
    May read in thee;
How small a part of time they share
That are so wondrous sweet and fair!

*Go, Lovely Rose,*
Edmund Waller

*While Byron, in his way as perverse as Cleopatra, dedicated his most perfect love poem to a boy:*

There be none of Beauty's daughters
    With a magic like thee;
And like music on the waters
    Is thy sweet voice to me:
When, as if its sound were causing
The charmed ocean's pausing,
The waves lie still and gleaming,
And the lull'd winds seem dreaming:
And the midnight moon is weaving
    Her bright chain o'er the deep;
Whose breast is gently heaving,
    As an infant's asleep:
So the spirit bows before thee,
To listen and adore thee;
With a full but soft emotion,
Like the swell of Summer's ocean.

*Stanzas for Music,*
Lord Byron

*Another rather conceited technique, employed by Spenser, is to tell the beloved that, although her beauty will not last for ever, you are conferring immortality on her by putting her in a poem. Faustus was more modest and said that Fair Helen was conferring immortality on him simply by giving him a kiss.*

One day I wrote her name upon the strand,
But came the waves and washed it away;
Again I wrote it with a second hand,
But came the tide and made my pains his prey.
Vain man, said she, that does in vain assay,
A mortal thing so to immortalize,
For I myself shall like to this decay,
And eke my name be wiped out likewise.
Not so, quoth I, let baser things devise
To die in dust, but you shall live by fame;
My verse your virtues rare shall eternize,
And in the heavens write your glorious name,
    Where when as death, shall all the world subdue,
    Our love shall live and later life renew.

*Sonnet LXXV* from *Amoretti*,
Edmund Spenser


Was this the face that launch'd a thousand ships
And burnt the topless towers of Ilium?
Sweet Helen, make me immortal with a kiss.
Her lips suck forth my soul; see where it flies! —
Come, Helen, come, give me my soul again,
Here will I dwell, for heaven be in these lips,
And all is dross that is not Helena.
I will be Paris, and for love of thee,
Instead of Troy, shall Wertenberg be sacked;
And I will combat with weak Menelaus,
And wear thy colours on my plumed crest:
Yea, I will wound Achilles in the heel,
And then return to Helen for a kiss.
Oh! thou art fairer than the evening air
Clad in the beauty of a thousand stars;
Brighter art thou than flaming Jupiter
When he appear'd to hapless Semele:

More lovely than the monarch of the sky
In wanton Arethusa's azur'd arms:
And none but thou shalt be my paramour.

from *Doctor Faustus*,
Christopher Marlowe

*When I was learning to type at Oxford, John Donne suddenly became fashionable, and every undergraduate without fail would quote 'Oh my America, my Newfoundland' before he pounced on one.*

Off with that girdle, like heaven's zone glistering
But a far fairer world encompassing.
Unpin that spangled breast-plate, which you wear
That th'eyes of busy fools may be stopped there:
Unlace yourself, for that harmonious chime
Tells me from you that now 'tis your bedtime.
Off with that happy busk, which I envy
That still can be and still can stand so nigh.
Your gown's going off such beauteous state reveals
As when from flowery meads th'hills shadow steals
Off with your wiry coronet and show
The hairy diadem which on you doth grow.

Off with those shoes: and then safely tread
In this love's hallowed temple, this soft bed.
In such white robes heaven's angels used to be
Perceived by men; thou Angel bring'st with thee
A heaven-like Mahomet's Paradise; and though
Ill spirits walk in white, we easily know
By this, these Angels from an evil sprite:
They set our hairs, but these our flesh upright.
  Licence my roving hands, and let them go
Behind, before, above, between, below.
Oh my America, my Newfoundland,

My kingdom, safest when with one man manned,
My mine of precious stones, my Empery,
How blessed am I in thus discovering thee.

*To his Mistress*, John Donne

## Seductions and Making Love

Now we come to sex proper and all its subsequent euphemisms: making love, or sleeping with people, or going to bed with them, call it what you will. For some people the first time can be a depressing experience. There isn't any love or bed in Brian Patten's poem, just a sordid coupling on the carpet after a party. And as with most unsuccessful one-night-stands, they couldn't wait to put as much distance as possible between each other afterwards. Roger McGough's gang-bang in a bus seems to have been a much jollier encounter. Occasionally, though, as in Edwin Morgan's Strawberries, the first pounce is suddenly transformed into something so perfect that all the senses are heightened, and the experience is never forgotten.

He said:
'Let's stay here
Now this place has emptied
& make gentle pornography with one another,
While the partygoers go out
& the dawn creeps in,
Like a stranger.

Let us not hesitate
Over what we know
Or over how cold this place has become,
But let's unclip our minds
And let tumble free
The mad, mangled crocodiles of love.'

So they did,
There among the woodbines and guinness stains,

And later he caught a bus and she a train,
And all there was between them then
was rain.

*Party Piece*, Brian Patten

When the busstopped suddenly to avoid
damaging a mother and child in the road, the
younglady in the greenhat sitting opposite
was thrown across me, and not being one to
miss an opportunity i started to makelove
with all my body.

At first she resisted saying that it
was tooearly in the morning and toosoon
after breakfast and that anyway she found
me repulsive. But when i explained that
this being a nuclearage, the world was going
to end at lunchtime, she tookoff her
greenhat, put her busticket in her pocket
and joined in the exercise.

The buspeople, and therewere many of
them, were shockedandsurprised and amused
andannoyed, but when the word got around
that the world was coming to an end at lunchtime, they put their pride in their pockets
with their bustickets and madelove one with
the other. And even the busconductor, being
over, climbed into the cab and stuck up
some sort of relationship with the driver.

Thatnight, on the bus coming home,
wewere all a little embarrassed, especially me
and the younglady in the greenhat, and we
all started to say different ways howhasty
and foolish we had been. Butthen, always
having been a bitofalad, i stood up and

said it was a pity that the world didn't nearly
end every lunchtime and that we could always
pretend. And then it happened . . .

Quick asa crash we all changed partners
and soon the bus was a quiver with white
mothballbodies doing naughty things.

And the next day
And everyday
In everybus
In everystreet
In everytown
In everycountry

people pretended that the world was coming
to an end at lunchtime. It still hasn't.
Although in a way it has.

At *Lunchtime A Story of Love*,
Roger McGough


There were never strawberries
like the ones we had
that sultry afternoon
sitting on the step
of the open french window
facing each other
your knees held in mine
the blue plates in our laps
the strawberries glistening
in the hot sunlight
we dipped them in sugar
looking at each other
not hurrying the feast
for one to come
the empty plates
laid on the stone together
with the two forks crossed

and I bent towards you
sweet in the air
in my arms
abandoned like a child
from your eager mouth
the taste of strawberries
in my memory
lean back again
let me love you

let the sun beat
on our forgetfulness
one hour of all
the heat intense
the summer lightning
on the Kilpatrick hills

let the storm wash the plates.

*Strawberries*, Edwin Morgan

*Lucky couple — the rain even did the washing up for them. If one goes into details about sexual encounters it is all too easy to sound smutty. Sir Charles Sedley escapes such a fate by being extremely funny, and by inspired use of suggestion. Chaucer and Rossetti are merely great poets:*

Young Corydon and Phyllis
Sat in a lovely grove,
Contriving crowns of lilies,
Repeating toys of love,
   And something else, but what I dare not name.

But as they were a-playing,
She ogled so the swain,
It saved her plainly saying
Let's kiss to ease our pain:
   And something else, but what I dare not name.

A thousand times he kissed her,
Laying her on the green;
But as he farther pressed her,
A pretty leg was seen;
    And something else, but what I dare not name.

So many beauties viewing,
His ardour still increased;
And greater joys pursuing,
He wandered o'er her breast:
    And something else, but what I dare not name.

A last effort she trying,
His passion to withstand;
Cried, but it was faintly crying,
Pray take away your hand:
    And something else, but what I dare not name.

Young Corydon grown bolder
The minutes would improve;
This is the time, he told her
To show you how I love;
    And something else, but what I dare not name.

The nymph seemed almost dying,
Dissolved in amorous heat;
She kissed him and told him sighing,
My dear your love is great:
    And something else, but what I dare not name.

But Phyllis did recover
Much sooner than the swain:
She blushing asked her lover,
Shall we not kiss again:
    And something else, but what I dare not name.

Thus Love his revels keeping,
'Til Nature at a stand;
From talk they fell to sleeping,

Holding each others hand;
   And something else, but what I dare not name.

*On the Happy Corydon and Phyllis*,
Sir Charles Sedley

Her slender arms, her soft and supple back,
Her tapered sides – all fleshly, smooth and white –
He stroked, and asked for favours at her neck,
Her snowish throat, her breasts so round and light;
Thus in this heaven he took his delight,
And smothered her with kisses upon kisses,
Till gradually he came to learn where bliss is.

from *Troilus and Criseyde*, Geoffrey Chaucer
Translated by Alan Bold

Why, Jenny, as I watch you there –
For all your wealth of loosened hair,
Your silk ungirdled and unlaced
And warm sweets open to the waist,
All golden in the lamplight's gleam –
You know not what a book you seem,
Half-read by lightning in a dream!

*Jenny*, Dante Gabriel Rossetti

*Sometimes women make the running. Elinor Glyn is carried along by gusto and sheer preposterousness. Here the 'mad, mangled crocodiles of love' referred to by Brian Patten, are joined by a purring tiger, and an undulating snake – rather like the London Zoo at feeding time. One is amazed that Paul managed to sleep through it all.*

A madness of tender caressing seized her. She purred as a tiger might have done, while she undulated like a snake. She touched him with her finger-tips, she kissed his throat, his wrists, the palms of his hands, his eyelids, his hair. Strange subtle kisses, unlike the kisses of women. And often, between her purrings, she murmured love-words in some fierce language of her own, brushing his ears and his eyes with her lips the while. And through it all, Paul slept on, the Eastern perfume in the air drugging his senses.

from *Three Weeks*, Elinor Glyn

*Few novelists write with more restraint about love than Anthony Powell. In this passage from* The Acceptance World, *the narrator, Nicholas Jenkins, is being driven down the Great West Road to a winter weekend in the country. He is sitting in the back under a rug with a married woman he has long wanted, but to whom he has given no indication of his feelings. The first time is often the best because of the novelty; because people usually try harder, and because of the sudden ecstatic awareness that, for the moment at least, one is desired as much as one desires. This, for me, is a particularly nostalgic piece, because in the days before the Chiswick flyover was built, the Great West Road at night used to be one of the great showpieces of London. As one drove out to the airport or to the country, each company building along the route had its own glittering advertising gimmick: the great Goodyear tyre, the sapphire wheel of Mercedes Benz, the eternally pouring golden Lucozade bottle, and, most beautiful of all, the Jantzen girl (referred to by Mr Powell) who dived in her red bathing dress over and over again throughout the night.*

*I started my career as a reporter in Brentford and Chiswick on a paper inappropriately called* The Middlesex Independent *and used often to work at night covering stories and narrowly avoiding being covered by other journalists. A lot of my time was spent traipsing up and down the Great West Road.*

Although not always simultaneous in taking effect, nor necessarily at all equal in voltage, the process of love is rarely unilateral. When the moment comes, a secret attachment is often returned with interest. Some know this by instinct; others learn in a hard school.

The exact spot must have been a few hundred yards beyond the point where the electrically illuminated young lady in a bathing-dress dives eternally through the petrol-tainted air; night and day, winter and summer, never reaching the water of the pool to which she endlessly glides. Like some image of arrested development she returns for ever, voluntarily, to the springboard from which she started her leap. A few seconds after I had seen this bathing belle journeying, as usual, imperturbably through the frozen air, I took Jean in my arms.

Her response, so sudden and passionate, seemed surprising only a minute or two later. All at once everything was changed. Her body felt at the same time hard and yielding, giving a kind of glow as if live current issued from it. I used to wonder afterwards whether, in the last resort, of all the time we spent together, however ecstatic, those first moments on the Great West Road were not the best...

We had bowled along much farther through the winter night, under cold, glittering stars, when Templar turned the car off the main road ... He drew up with a jerk in front of the door, the wheels churning up the snow. He climbed quickly from his seat, and went round to the back of the car, to unload from the boot some eatables and wine they had brought from London. At the same moment Mona came out of her sleep or coma. With the rug still wrapped round her, she jumped out of her side of the car, and ran across the Sisley landscape to the front door, which someone had opened from within. As she ran she gave a series of little shrieks of agony at the cold. Her footprints left deep marks on the face of the drive, where the snow lay soft and tender, like the clean, clean sheets of a measureless bed.

'Where shall I find you?'

'Next to you on the left.'

'How soon?'

'Give it half an hour.'

'I'll be there.'

'Don't be too long.'

She laughed softly when she said that, disengaging herself from the rug that covered both of us.

from *The Acceptance World*, Anthony Powell

# The Joys of Loving

We turn to the aftermath of love-making. When there has been no love involved, the experience is a cheerless one, described marvellously by Philip Larkin as bursting into 'Fulfilment's desolate attic'. In Auden's poem, however, we find a feeling of contentment and security:

> Warm are the still and lucky miles,
> White shores of longing stretch away,
> The light of recognition fills
> The whole great day, and bright
> The tiny world of lovers' arms.
>
> Silence invades the breathing wood
> Where drowsy limbs a treasure keep
> Now greenly falls the learned shade
> Across the sleeping brows
> And stirs their secret to a smile.
>
> Restored! Returned! The lost are borne
> On seas of shipwreck home at last:
> See! In the fire of praising burns
> The dry dumb past, and we
> The life-day long shall part no more.
>
> *Song*, W. H. Auden

Browning once said that the meanest of God's creatures boasts two sides to him, one to face the world with, one to show a woman when he loved her. One of the good things above love is that it suddenly redeems the most unlikely people like the couple in the Bath teashop:

'Let us not speak, for the love we bear one another —
    Let us hold hands and look.'
She, such a very ordinary little woman;
    He, such a thumping crook;
But both, for a moment, little lower than the angels
    In the teashop's ingle-nook.

*In a Bath Teashop*, John Betjeman

*Another of the joys of being loved by someone you love is that it makes you feel all-powerful. Here we see even one of P. G. Wodehouse's silly asses beginning to think he's rather a good show, while John Donne's égoïsme à deux almost reaches megalomania. This was the first poem of Donne's I ever read. I was totally entranced by it. I remember saying the lines 'She's all States, and all Princes I; nothing else is' over and over again. I was so envious of people who could feel sure enough of each other to say that.*

'Bill, are you really fond of me?'
    'Fond of you!'
    She gave a sigh. 'You're so splendid!'
    Bill was staggered. Those were strange words. He had never thought much of himself. He had always looked on himself as rather a chump – well-meaning, perhaps, but an awful ass! It seemed incredible that anyone, and Elizabeth of all people, could look on him as splendid.
    And yet the very fact that she had said it gave it a plausible sort of sound. It shook his convictions. Splendid! Was he? By Jove, perhaps he was, what? Rum idea, but it grew on a chap. Filled with a novel feeling of exaltation, he kissed Elizabeth eleven times in rapid succession.
    He felt devilish fit. He would have liked to run a mile or two and jump a few gates. He felt grand and strong and full of beans. What a ripping thing life was when you came to think of it.

from *Uneasy Money*, P. G. Wodehouse

Busy old fool, unruly Sun,
   Why dost thou thus,
Through windows and through curtains call on us?
Must to thy motions lovers' seasons run?
   Saucy, pedantic wretch, go chide
   Late school-boys, and sour 'prentices,
Go tell Court-huntsmen that the King will ride,
Call country ants to harvest offices,
Love, all alike, no season knows, nor clime,
Nor hours, days, months, which are the rags of time.

   Thy beams, so reverend and strong
   Why shouldst thou think?
I could eclipse and cloud them with a wink,
But that I would not lose her sight so long;
   If her eyes have not blinded thine,
   Look, and tomorrow late tell me,
Whether both the Indias of spice and mine
Be where thou left'st them, or lie here with me.
Ask for those kings whom thou saw'st yesterday,
And thou shalt hear, 'All here in one bed lay.'

   She's all States, and all Princes I;
   Nothing else is.
Princes do but play us; compared to this,
All honour's mimic; all wealth alchemy.
   Thou, Sun, art half as happy as we,
   In that the world's contracted thus:
Thine age asks ease, and since thy duties be
To warm the world, that's done in warming us.
Shine here to us, and thou art everywhere;
This bed thy centre is, these walls thy sphere.

                *The Sun Rising*, John Donne

# Parting

Trying to stop the clock is, of course, a common pastime of lovers. I remember lying in bed in the morning watching my husband dress, wondering how on earth I'd survive until I saw him that evening, employing every kind of subterfuge like hiding his shoes or his cuff-links to delay him. Juliet, after a night of love with Romeo, tried the same technique rather more successfully:

> Juliet: Wilt thou be gone? it is not yet near day:
>    It was the nightingale, and not the lark,
>    That pierc'd the fearful hollow of thine ear;
>    Nightly she sings on yon pomegranate tree:
>    Believe me, love, it was the nightingale.
> Romeo: It was the lark, the herald of the morn,
>    No nightingale: look, love, that envious streaks
>    Do lace the severing clouds in yonder east:
>    Night's candles are burnt out, and jocund day
>    Stands tiptoe on the misty mountain tops: ·
>    I must be gone and live, or stay and die.
> Juliet: Yon light is not daylight, I know it, I:
>    It is some meteor that the sun exhales
>    To be to thee this night a torch-bearer,
>    And light thee on thy way to Mantua:
>    Therefore stay yet, thou need'st not to be gone.
> Romeo: Let me be ta'en, let me be put to death;
>    I am content, so thou wilt have it so.
>    I'll say yon gray is not the morning's eye,
>    'Tis the pale reflex of Cynthia's brow;
>    Nor that is not the lark whose notes do beat
>    The vaulty heaven so high above our heads:

I have more care to stay than will to go —
Come, death and welcome! Juliet wills it so —
How is't my soul? let's talk; it is not day.

from *Romeo and Juliet*,
William Shakespeare

*I've always thought one of the most haunting titles for a novel was John Braine's* Stay with Me till Morning. *It reminds me of Swinburne's equally haunting and beautiful lines:*

I turn to thee as some green afternoon
Turns toward sunset, and is loth to die;
Ah God, ah God, that day should be so soon!

*John Donne wrote much in the same vein:*

The day breaks not: it is my heart,
Because that you and I must part.

*There is no doubt that the unhappiness of parting has inspired some marvellous poems. A. E. Housman, a repressed homosexual, seems to have suffered more bitterly from unrequited love than any other poet. Here he and Coventry Patmore explore the same theme: the world is round, so if you part from your lover and keep walking you'll eventually meet up round the back. Housman's poem, however, seems slightly the better one, perhaps because the sense of loss is more acute:*

White in the moon the long road lies,
    The moon stands blank above;
White in the moon the long road lies
    That leads me from my love.

Still hangs the hedge without a gust,
    Still, still the shadows stay:
My feet upon the moonlit dust
    Pursue the ceaseless way.

The world is round, so travellers tell,
    And straight though reach the track,
Trudge on, trudge on, 'twill all be well,
    The way will guide one back.

But ere the circle homeward hies
    Far, far must it remove:
White in the moon the long road lies
    That leads me from my love.

from *A Shropshire Lad*, A. E. Housman

With all my will, but much against my heart,
We two now part.
My Very Dear,
Our solace is, the sad road lies so clear.
It needs no art,
With faint, averted feet
And many a tear,
In our opposèd paths to persevere.
Go thou to East, I West.
We will not say
There's any hope, it is so far away.
But, O, my Best,
When the one darling of our widowhead,
The nursling Grief,
Is dead,
And no dews blur our eyes
To see the peach-bloom come in evening skies,
Perchance we may,
Where now this night is day,
And even through faith of still averted feet,
Making full circle of our banishment,
Amazèd meet;
The bitter journey to the bourne so sweet
Seasoning the termless feast of our content
With tears of recognition never dry.

*A Farewell*, Coventry Patmore

*One of the characteristics of love is the infinitely tender and protective attitude one has towards the loved one while she or he is away:*

> Her Eyes the Glow-worme lend thee,
> The Shooting Starres attend thee;
>    And the Elves also,
>    Whose little eyes glow,
> Like the sparks of fire, befriend thee.
>
> No *Will-o'-th'-Wispe* mis-light thee;
> Nor Snake, or Slow-worme bite thee:
>    But on, on thy way
>    Not making a stay,
> Since Ghost ther's none to affright thee.
>
> Let not the darke thee cumber;
> What though the Moon do's slumber?
>    The Starres of the night
>    Will lend thee their light,
> Like Tapers cleare without number.
>
> Then *Julia* let me wooe thee,
> Thus, thus to come unto me:
>    And when I shall meet
>    Thy silv'ry feet,
> My soule Ile poure into thee.

   *The Night-Piece, to* Julia, Robert Herrick


> A pity beyond all telling
> Is hid in the heart of love:
> The folk who are buying and selling;
> The clouds on their journey above;
> The cold wet winds ever blowing;
> And the shadowy hazel grove
> Where mouse-grey waters are flowing,
> Threaten the head that I love.

   *The Pity of Love*, W. B. Yeats

*Next we come to a much admired poem by Richard Lovelace, about a soldier going to the war and leaving his girlfriend behind. Maybe he was fed up with her chastity and wanted to romp with a few less virtuous camp-followers. It always seems a very unflattering poem to me. Nor, if I'd been Lucasta, would I have liked him admitting he loved his honour more than me so publicly. Perhaps Lovelace realized this, and slipped in such endearments as 'sweet' and 'dear' in brackets to soften her up. I much prefer the brief, exquisite plea of the anonymous sailor for the West Wind to return, and waft his ship home to port, a warm bed, and his beloved.*

Tell me not (Sweet) I am unkind,
    That from the nunnery
Of thy chaste breast, and quiet mind,
    To war and arms I fly.

True, a new mistress now I chase,
    The first foe in the field;
And with a stronger faith embrace
    A sword, a horse, a shield.

Yet this inconstancy is such,
    As thou too shall adore,
I could not love thee (Dear) so much,
    Lov'd I not honour more.

*To Lucasta, going to the Wars,*
Richard Lovelace

Western Wind, when wilt thou blow,
    The small rain down can rain?
Christ, if my love were in my arms
    And I in my bed again!

Anon

*We have talked about lovers who've been parted unwillingly by wars or circumstances. Now we come to one half of the couple enforcing the separation. Yeats asks his mistress to*

*pack it in before the whole thing goes completely sour. In* The
Last Ride Together *Browning has been given his marching
orders by a mistress who likes him but admits she can never
love him. His mood at the moment is ecstatic, his mistress is
still with him, he is revelling in the relief of a decision having
been made and a sense of behaving frightfully well. He is also
probably suffering from shock. The morning after, one feels,
would have been absolutely frightful; his mistress would have
gone, and the pain would really begin to hurt.*

Autumn is over the long leaves that love us,
And over the mice in the barley sheaves;
Yellow the leaves of the rowan above us,
And yellow the wet wild-strawberry leaves.

The hour of the waning of love has beset us,
And weary and worn are our sad souls now;
Let us part, ere the season of passion forget us,
With a kiss and a tear on thy drooping brow.

*The Falling of the Leaves*, W. B. Yeats

I SAID — Then, dearest, since 'tis so,
Since now at length my fate I know,
Since nothing all my love avails,
Since all my life seemed meant for fails,
    Since this was written and needs must be —
My whole heart rises up to bless
Your name in pride and thankfulness!
Take back the hope you gave, — I claim
Only a memory of the same,
— And this beside, if you will not blame,
    Your leave for one more last ride with me.

My mistress bent that brow of hers;
Those deep dark eyes where pride demurs
When pity would be softening through,
Fixed me a breathing-while or two
    With life or death in the balance — Right!

The blood replenished me again;
My last thought was at least not vain:
I and my mistress, side by side
Shall be together, breathe and ride,
So, one day more am I deified.
    Who knows but the world may end to-night?

Hush! if you saw some western cloud
All billowy-bosomed, over-bowed
By many benedictions — sun's
And moon's and evening star's at once —
    And so, you, looking and loving best,
Conscious grew, your passion drew
Cloud, sunset, moonrise, star-shine too,
Down on you, near and yet more near,
Till flesh must fade for heaven was here! —
Thus leant she and linger'd — joy and fear!
    Thus lay she a moment on my breast.

Then we began to ride. My soul
Smoothed itself out, a long-cramped scroll
Freshening and fluttering in the wind.
Past hopes already lay behind.
    What need to strive with a life awry?
Had I said that, had I done this,
So might I gain, so might I miss.
Might she have loved me? just as well
She might have hated, who can tell!
Where had I been now if the worst befell?
    And here we are riding, she and I.
. . . .
What does it all mean, poet? Well,
Your brains beat into rhythm, you tell
What we felt only; you expressed
You hold things beautiful the best,
    And pace them in rhyme so, side by side.
'Tis something, nay 'tis much: but then,

Have you yourself what's best for men?
And you – poor, sick, old ere your time –
Nearer one whit your own sublime
Than we who never have turned a rhyme?
Sing, riding's a joy! For me, I ride.

from *The Last Ride Together*,
Robert Browning

## Kissing The Joy as It Flies

*The problem about love is that it never stands still. In a good relationship those ecstatic, frenetic, first few weeks mellow into something just as tender, but calmer and more durable. What has haunted writers over the years is how best to appreciate these blissful interludes when they come, and how to cope when they loose their intensity, or end in loss and tragedy. Enjoy but don't cling on, seems to be the message. Sensible advice no doubt, but extremely hard to follow.*

O love, be fed with apples while you may,
And feel the sun and go in royal array,
A smiling innocent on the heavenly causeway.

Though in what listening horror for the cry
That soars in outer blackness dismally,
The dumb blind beast, the paranoic fury,

Be warm, enjoy the season, lift your head,
Exquisite in the pulse of tainted blood,
That shivering glory not to be despised.

Take your delight in momentariness,
Walk between dark and dark, a shining space
With the grave's narrowness, though not its peace.

*O Love in Me*, Robert Graves

He who bends to himself a Joy
Doth the winged life destroy;
But he who kisses the Joy as it flies
Lives in Eternity's sunrise.

from *To God*, William Blake

Tears, idle tears, I know not what they mean,
Tears from the depth of some divine despair
Rise in the heart, and gather to the eyes,
In looking in the happy Autumn-fields,
And thinking of the days that are no more.

. . . .

Dear as remember'd kisses after death,
And sweet as those by hopeless fancy feign'd
On lips that are for others; deep as love,
Deep as first love, and wild with all regret,
O Death in Life, the days that are no more.

> Song from *The Princess*,
> Alfred, Lord Tennyson

But when the melancholy fit shall fall
    Sudden from heaven like a weeping cloud,
That fosters the droop-headed flowers all,
    And hides the green hill in an April shroud;
Then glut thy sorrow on a morning rose,
    Or on the rainbow of the salt sand-wave,
    Or on the wealth of globèd peonies;
Or if thy mistress some rich anger shows,
    Emprison her soft hand, and let her rave,
    And feed deep, deep upon her peerless eyes.

She dwells with Beauty — Beauty that must die;
    And Joy, whose hand is ever at his lips
Bidding adieu; and aching Pleasure nigh,
    Turning to Poison while the bee-mouth sips:
Ay, in the very temple of delight
    Veil'd Melancholy has her sovran shrine,
Though seen of none save him whose strenuous tongue
Can burst Joy's grape against his palate fine;
    His soul shall taste the sadness of her might,
    And be among her cloudy trophies hung.

> from *Ode to Melancholy*, John Keats

# The Unlucky

*We have talked about love that is at least temporarily reciprocated. But what about the girls who never get anyone, who struggle home on the tube or train to lonely flats, to gas-ring suppers for one, with no prospect of a lover to cherish or cheer them up?*

From the geyser ventilators
    Autumn winds are blowing down
On a thousand business women
    Having baths in Camden Town.

Waste pipes chuckle into runnels,
    Steam's escaping here and there,
Morning trains through Camden cutting
    Shake the Crescent and the Square.

Early nip of changeful autumn,
    Dahlias glimpsed through garden doors,
At the back precarious bathrooms
    Jutting out from upper floors;

And behind their frail partitions
    Business women lie and soak,
Seeing through the draughty skylight
    Flying clouds and railway smoke.

Rest you there, poor unbelov'd ones,
    Lap your loneliness in heat.
All too soon the tiny breakfast,
    Trolley-bus and windy street!

*Business Girls*, John Betjeman

*Poor Charlotte Brontë was probably just as vulnerable as one of those girls. Sent out to Belgium to learn French, she fell hopelessly in love with her professor. He was the first man other than her father and brother she had really known, and it took only a rather impersonal kindness on his part to unloose all the dark Brontë passion bottled up inside her. Back home, she found it impossible to forget him – showing that when there is nothing else to take its place, love will survive on the meagrest fare.*

Day and night I find neither rest nor peace. If I sleep I am disturbed by tormenting dreams in which I see you, always severe, always grave, always incensed against me. Forgive me then, Monsieur, if I adopt the course of writing to you again. How can I endure life if I make no effort to ease its sufferings? . . .

Monsieur, the poor have not need of much to sustain them – they ask only for the crumbs that fall from the rich men's table. But if they are refused they die of hunger. Nor do I either, need much affection from those I love... But you showed me of yore a *little* interest, when I was your pupil in Brussels, and I hold on to the maintenance of that *little* interest – I hold on to it as I would hold on to life.

(*Nearly a year later*) I tell you frankly that I have tried meanwhile to forget you . . . I have done everything; I have sought occupations; I have denied myself absolutely the pleasure of speaking about you – even to Emily; but I have been able to conquer neither my regrets nor my impatience . . . To write to an old pupil cannot be a very interesting occupation for you, I know; but for me it is life. Your last letter was stay and prop to me – nourishment to me for half a year . . . To forbid me to write to you, to refuse to answer me, would be to tear from me my only joy on earth, to deprive me of my last privilege... When day by day I await a letter, and when day by day disappointment comes to fling me back into overwhelming sorrow, and the sweet delight of seeing your handwriting and reading your counsel escapes me . . . then fever claims me – I lose appetite and sleep – I pine away.          *Letter*, Charlotte Brontë

*Very often women who are starved of love form an attachment for a homosexual man. I, myself, in my very early twenties, was crazy about a bronzed and golden-haired account executive with a profile like a Roman coin. He used to take me to the theatre or the ballet once or twice a week, and because he didn't pounce, and only wanted to hold my hand or stroke my hair occasionally, I assumed he was serious about me. Shortly afterwards he shacked up with another man. In the following extract, Barbara Pym's charming but somewhat naive married heroine misconstrues Piers' feelings towards her:*

May has always seemed to me, as indeed it has to poets, the most romantic of all the months. There are so many days when the air is really like wine – a delicate white wine, perhaps Vouvray drunk on the banks of the Loire. This afternoon had about it something of the quality of that day when Piers and I had walked through the Temple and seen the cat crouching among the tulips and the new leaves covering up the old sad fruits on the fig tree.

I was wearing a dress of deep coral-coloured poplin, very simple, with a pair of coral and silver earrings, and a bracelet to match. I always like myself in deep clear colours, and I felt at my best now and wondered if people were looking at me as I passed them. They seemed to be mostly lovers – absorbed in each other, and I did not mind this, but when a drab-looking woman in a tweed skirt and crumpled pink blouse looked up from her sandwich and *New Statesman*, I felt suddenly embarrassed and was reminded of poor Miss Limpsett in Piers's office. What could her life have held? What future was there for her and the woman in the crumpled pink blouse?

I was glad when I reached our meeting place and saw Piers standing with his back to me, apparently absorbed in a border of lupins. I wanted to rush up to him with some silly extravagant gesture, like covering his eyes with my hands; and my hands were outstretched, waiting to be taken in his, when I called his name and he turned round to face me.

'I hope I'm not late,' I said, discarding as one does the other more exciting openings I had prepared.

'Not very,' he said, evading my outstretched hands without seeming to do so in any obvious way. 'You look very charming. That colour suits you.'

I had hoped he would say this, but I was pleased when the words actually came. We stood for a few moments looking at the lupins.

'How I should love to get right in among them and smell their warm peppery smell!' I said exuberantly. 'I do so adore it!'

'My dear, it isn't quite you, this enthusiasm,' said Piers. 'You must be cool and dignified, and behave perfectly in character – not plunging in among lupins.'

'Oh.' I was a little cast down. 'Is that how I am – cool and dignified? I don't mind being thought elegant, of course – but cool and dignified. It doesn't sound very lovable.'

'Lovable? Is that how you want to be?' He sounded surprised.

'I should have thought everyone did on this sort of an afternoon,' I said, rather at a loss. It was evident that his mood did not quite match mine, and that I should have to – as women nearly always must – damp down my own exuberant happiness until we were more nearly in sympathy.

'Wilmet, what's the matter with you? You're talking like one of the cheaper women's magazines.' Piers's tone was rather petulant.

Love is the cheapest of all emotions, I thought; or such a universal one that it makes one talk like a cheap magazine. What, indeed, was the matter with me?

'I shouldn't have thought *you'd* know much about those,' I said.

'We don't read them at the press, certainly, but one sees them somehow. Have we been long enough at these lupins? Shall we walk on?'

'Yes,' I said, for I could think of nothing else to say.

'Poor girl,' he said teasingly, after we had been walking in silence for some time. 'Don't mind my ill-humour. You said yourself that I was a moody person.'

. . . .

'Now, Wilmet, what would you like to do next? Go to the pictures, have a nice sit down in a deckchair, or what?'

'I should like to see where you live,' I said firmly.

'All right. Tea at home then. But don't expect too much. We must get a bus to Shepherd's Bush first of all.'

. . . .

'Will your colleague be at home this afternoon?' I asked, as we stood on an island amid a swirl of trolley buses.

'My colleague?'

'The person you share the flat with.'

'Oh, of course. Yet it's quite likely he'll be doing the week-end shopping at this very minute.'

We walked along a street full of cheap garish looking dress shops, their windows crammed with blouses and skirts in crude colours, and butchers' and greengrocers' smelling sickly in the heat. When we came to a grocer's, Piers went into the doorway and looked inside.

'Yes, there he is,' he said.

We went into the shop. I had imagined that I would imme- diately recognize the colleague when I saw him, but although there were several people at the counter none of them seemed quite right. There were two men and three women, two elderly and the other young and flashily dressed with dyed golden hair and long earrings. Surely, I wondered in horror, it couldn't be her? But no, Piers had said 'he', so it must be one of the non- descript looking men.

'Oh there you are — I thought we'd probably find you here.'

Piers had gone over into a corner where a small dark young man wearing black jeans and a blue tartan shirt, whom I had not noticed before, was peering into some biscuit tins.

'Wilmet, this is Keith — I don't think you've met before,' said Piers in a rather jolly tone which did not seem quite natural to him.

Keith gave a stiff little bow and looked at me warily. He was about twenty-five years old, with a neat-featured, rather appealing face and sombre brown eyes. His hair was cropped very short in the fashionable style of the moment. I noticed that it glistened like the wet fur of an animal.

'No, we haven't actually met, but I've heard a lot about you, Mrs Forsyth,' he said politely.

'I think we've spoken on the telephone, haven't we?' I said, recognizing the flat, rather common little voice as the one which had answered me the evening I had tried to ring up Piers. I could not reciprocate by saying that I had heard a lot about him, when I had heard nothing whatsoever. Indeed, I was so taken aback and confused by the encounter that I did not know what to say or even what to think. I stood rather awkwardly, my hand mechanically stroking a large black and white cat which was asleep on a sack of lentils. So *this* was the colleague.

Keith turned to Piers with some question about bacon.

'What do you think, Wilmet?' asked Piers. 'Which is the best kind of bacon?'

'I don't know,' I said, unable to give my attention to bacon. 'It depends what you like.'

'These two gentlemen will never make up their minds,' said the motherly looking woman behind the counter. 'I have to help them choose every time. Now what's the matter with that, dear?' she said to Keith. 'Is it too fat for your liking?'

'We like it more striped, as it were,' said Piers.

'*Striped*! Isn't that sweet – did you ever!' She turned to me. 'You mean *streaky*, dear – that's what we call it. Let me cut you some off there – this is nice.' She thrust a side of bacon towards us and then placed it in the machine.

It began to go backwards and forwards with a swishing noise, while the three of us stood in silence watching it. There was an air of unreality about the whole scene – Keith, with his absurd clothes, and bristly hair like a hedgehog or porcupine, was almost a comic figure. And yet I felt sad, too, as if something had come to an end.

from *A Glass of Blessings*, Barbara Pym

♥
♥
♥

# Escaping

*When one doesn't have a man, one often compensates by reading about romance. I've always felt reading romantic novels was a bit like eating a whole box of chocolates, or going to bed with a rotter. You can't stop during the act because it's so nice, but afterwards you wish you hadn't.*

*In my courting days when things were going badly, I used to get through four romances a day, devouring one after another: take one every four hours for the alleviation of heartache.*

*A favourite setting for romantic novelists, of course, is the desert. Time and again the heroine sets out alone in the midday sun, is apprehended by some mysterious Arab full of Eastern promise who whisks her off to the Dunes. But after a good deal of Sheik Rattle and Roll, he turns out to be no Arab:*

Gradually the terrible shuddering passed and the gasping sobs died away, and she lay still, so still and white that he was afraid ... the colour stole back slowly into her face and the little tremulous smile curved her lips. She slid her arm up and down his neck drawing his head down. 'I am not afraid,' she murmured slowly. 'I am not afraid of anything with your arms round me, my desert lover. Ahmed! Monseigneur.'

from *The Sheik*, E. M. Hull

*Sometimes authoresses cheated over their heroes:*

Ann caught her breath. The second outrider was bareheaded. That in itself was sufficiently interesting in this galaxy of turbans. But the bare head was blond. Burned-blond the colour of August corn. Berber Arabs could be light-complexioned, Ann

knew. But not this colour. No Berber could have that inso-
lently easy square-jawed face, that blunt straight nose, that
quietly humorous mouth above a dogged chin. This man looked
English! . . . He *is* an Englishman, she decided with queer
mounting excitement, for only an Englishman would have rid-
den so spirited a mount without the help of spurs.

from *To Win a Paradise*, Elizabeth Hoy

## Hommes Fatals et Femmes Fatales

*Arab Sheiks then certainly had lashings of sex appeal; now they've only got cash.* In real life there are the Hommes Fatals, *the havoc makers who attract far too effortlessly, leaving a trail of destruction in their wake. You meet one, vow not to get involved; the next moment you're being pulled into the quicksand and it's too late to escape. 'Enter these enchanted woods, you who dare,' wrote George Meredith.*

*The trouble with this kind of man is that he thrives on variety. 'I must have women,' he cries, like Macheath, 'There is nothing unbends the mind like them.' But as soon as he meets constancy, or things get heavy or tedious, he moves on to fresh fields like Matthew Arnold's cuckoo, and because there are always women waiting to tell him how wonderful he is, he tends to be rather smug. Often he is also petrified of get- ting involved like* The Indifferent *in John Donne's poem.*

> So have I heard the cuckoo's parting cry,
> From the wet field, through the vext garden-trees,
> Come with the volleying rain and tossing breeze:
> *The bloom is gone, and with the bloom go I.*
>
> from *Thyrsis*, Matthew Arnold

I can love both fair and brown,
　Her whom abundance melts, and her whom want betrays,
　Her who loves loneness best, and her who masks and plays,
　Her whom the country formed, and whom the town,
　Her who believes, and her who tries,
　Her who still weeps with spongy eyes,
　And her who is dry cork, and never cries;
　I can love her, and her, and you and you,
　I can love any, so she be not true.

Will no other vice content you?
Will it not serve your turn to do as did your mothers?
Or have you all old vices spent, and now would find out
     others?
Or doth a fear, that men are true, torment you?
Oh we are not, be not you so,
Let me, and do you, twenty know.
Rob me, but bind me not, and let me go.
Must I, who came to travail through you
Grow your fixed subject, because you are true?

Venus heard me sigh this song,
And by Love's sweetest part, Variety, she swore
She heard not this till now; and that it should be so no more.
She went, examined, and returned ere long,
And said, alas. Some two or three
Poor heretics in love there be,
Which think to 'stablish dangerous constancy.
But I have told them, since you will be true,
You shall be true to them, who are false to you.

*The Indifferent*, John Donne

'Rob me, but bind me not, and let me go', cried the Indifferent.
Shelley would have agreed with him. In the first of the next
two poems, he affirms that men are much better off if not
bogged down by boring monogamy. I suspect that Shelley is
ultimately rather an arid and unsatisfying poet because he is
more interested in ideas than people, and because he was incapable of sustaining any real passion. In the second poem,
Kipling's lusty lover has a girl in every port and frontier post.
I am particularly fond of this poem because it shows how
poetry can bring people together, and what pleasure is gained
by sharing it. There is an extremely attractive woman to whom
I talk occasionally when she walks her golden retrievers on
the Common. Last time we met, I was admiring the evening
primroses in Barnes Graveyard, she in turn admired my new

*mongrel, and asked its name. When I said that it was called Mabel, she promptly launched into The Lovers' Litany:*

> 'Mabel', 'Officers', 'Goodbye',
> Glamour, wine and witchery –
> On my soul's sincerity,
> *'Love like ours can never die!'*

*Unfamiliar with the poem, I looked it up when I got home, and then went on to read Rudyard Kipling's poem about General Bangs and his lecherous junketings, which I have included later in this book.*

> I never was attached to that great sect,
> Whose doctrine is, that each one should select
> Out of the crowd a mistress or a friend,
> And all the rest, though fair and wise, commend
> To cold oblivion, though it is in the code
> Of modern morals, and the beaten road
> Which those poor slaves with weary footsteps tread,
> Who travel to their home among the dead
> By the broad highway of the world, and so
> With one chained friend, perhaps a jealous foe,
> The dreariest and the longest journey go.
>
> > from *Epipsychidion*,
> > Percy Bysshe Shelley

> Eyes of grey – a sodden quay,
>     Driving rain and falling tears,
> As the steamer wears to sea
> In a parting storm of cheers.
>     Sing, for Faith and Hope are high –
>     None so true as you and I –
>     Sing the Lovers' Litany: –
>     *'Love like ours can never die!'*

> Eyes of Black – a throbbing keel,
> Milky foam to left and right;

Whispered converse near the wheel
In the brilliant tropic night.
  Cross that rules the Southern Sky!
  Stars that sweep, and wheel, and fly,
  Hear the Lovers' Litany: —
  *'Love like ours can never die!'*


Eyes of brown — a dusty plain
Split and parched with heat of June,
Flying hoof and tightened rein,
Hearts that beat the old, old tune.
  Side by side the horses fly,
  Frame we now the old reply
  Of the Lovers' Litany: —
  *'Love like ours can never die!'*


Eyes of blue — the Simla Hills
Silvered with the moonlight hoar;
Pleading of the waltz that thrills,
Dies and echoes round Benmore.
  *'Mabel,' 'Officers,' 'Good-bye,'*
  Glamour, wine and witchery —
  On my soul's sincerity,
  *'Love like ours can never die!'*


Maidens, of your charity,
Pity my most luckless state.
Four times Cupid's debtor I —
Bankrupt in quadruplicate.
  Yet, despite this evil case,
  As a maiden showed me grace,
  Four-and-forty times would I
  Sing the Lovers' Litany: —
  *'Love like ours can never die!'*

*The Lovers' Litany*,
Rudyard Kipling

*Havoc makers are easily irritated by any display of possessiveness in their girlfriends. But if you love someone it's terribly difficult not to be jealous. For as Donne points out when he's stopped being Indifferent:*

> Oh if thou carest not whom I love,
> Alas thou lovest not me.

*Anyone, however, who has a boy friend who runs around with other girls, will sympathize with poor Cloe's predicament in the next poem, although the beauty of Matthew Prior's penultimate verse must almost have compensated for any infidelity. Artists and writers, of course, are hellish people to be in love with because they can always justify any lapse in behaviour by saying they were searching for material.*

Dear Cloe, how blubber'd is that pretty Face?
    The Cheek all on Fire, and Thy Hair all uncurl'd:
Pr'ythee quit this Caprice; and (as Old FALSTAFF says)
    Let Us e'en talk a little like Folks of This World.

How canst Thou presume, Thou hast leave to destroy
    The Beauties, which VENUS but lent to Thy Keeping?
Those Looks were design'd to inspire Love and Joy:
    More ord'nary Eyes may serve People for weeping.

To be vext at a Trifle or two that I writ,
    Your Judgment at once, and my Passion You wrong:
You take that for Fact, which will scarce be found Wit:
    Od's Life! must One swear to the Truth of a Song?

What I speak, my fair *Cloe*, and what I write, shews
    The Diff'rence there is betwixt Nature and Art:
I court others in Verse; but I love Thee in Prose;
    And They have my Whimsies; but Thou hast my Heart.

The God of us Verse-men (You know Child) the SUN,
  How after his Journeys He sets up his Rest:
If at Morning o'er Earth 'tis his Fancy to run;
  At Night he reclines on his THETIS's Breast.

So when I am weary'd with wand'ring all Day;
  To Thee my Delight in the Evening I come:
No matter what Beauties I saw in my Way:
  They were but my Visits; but Thou art my Home.

Then finish, dear Cloe, this Pastoral War;
  And let us like HORACE and LYDIA agree:
For Thou art a Girl as much brighter than Her,
  As He was a Poet sublimer than Me.

*A Better Answer*, Matthew Prior

*Female havoc makers can be even more formidable. 'So may your mighty, amazing, beauty move, envy in all women, and in all men, love,' wrote John Donne. We all know the type and don't invite her to our parties. Like Keats' temptress she seems so frail and innocent a man longs to protect her, only to discover the moment he's totally enslaved that she's about as vulnerable as a boa constrictor.*

I met a lady in the meads,
  Full beautiful – a faery's child,
Her hair was long, her foot was light,
  And her eyes were wild.

I made a garland for her head,
  And bracelets too, and fragrant zone;
She look'd at me as she did love,
  And made sweet moan.

I set her on my pacing steed
  And nothing else saw all day long,
For sidelong would she bend, and sing
  A faery's song.

She found me roots of relish sweet
    And honey wild and manna dew,
And sure in language strange she said,
    'I love thee true.'

She took me to her elfin grot,
    And there she wept and sigh'd full sore,
And there I shut her wild wild eyes
    With kisses four.

And there she lulled me asleep,
    And there I dream'd – Ah! woe betide!
The latest dream I ever dream'd
    On the cold hill side.

I saw pale kings and princes too,
    Pale warriors, death-pale were they all,
They cried – 'La belle Dame sans Merci
    Hath thee in thrall!'

I saw their starved lips in the gloam
    With horrid warning gaped wide,
And I awoke and found me here,
    On the cold hill side.

And this is why I sojourn here
    Alone and palely loitering,
Though the sedge is wither'd from the lake
    And no birds sing.

                  from *La Belle Dame sans Merci*,
                         John Keats

*Alone and palely loitering with intent. A friend of mine said that one of Shelley's more decorative abandoned girl friends ought to have been called La Belle Dame Sans Percy. The same night another friend commented that Rosy-fingered Dawn sounded just like three o'clock in the morning at a Lesbian night club. But enough of such punning. The cruel thing about beauty is that it enables those who possess it to treat people like dirt, then whistle them back again. Both Shakespeare and Milton had bitter words to say on the subject:*

> Take, O take those lips away,
>   That so sweetly were forsworn;
> And those eyes, the break of day,
>   Lights that do mislead the morn:
> But my kisses bring again, bring again
> Seals of love, but seal'd in vain, seal'd in vain.
>
> from *Measure for Measure*,
> William Shakespeare

> Yet beauty, though injurious, hath strange power,
> After offence returning, to regain
> Love once possess'd.
>
> from *Samson Agonistes*, John Milton

*If, on the other hand, you put people on the rack for long enough, obsessive love turns to black corroding hatred.*

> When thou must home to shades of underground,
> And there arrived, a newe admirèd guest,
> The beauteous spirits do engirt thee round,
> White Iope, blithe Helen, and the rest,
> To hear the stories of thy finish'd love
> From that smoothe tongue whose music hell can move;
>
> Then wilt thou speake of banqueting delights,
> Of masks and revels which sweete youth did make,
> Of journeys and great challenges of knights,
> And all these triumphs for thy beauty's sake:
> When thou has told these honours done to thee,
> Then tell, O tell, how thou didst murder me.
>
> *Vobiscum est Iope*, Thomas Campion

Remember thee! remember thee!
    Till Lethe quench life's burning stream
Remorse and shame shall cling to thee,
    And haunt thee like a feverish dream!

Remember thee! Aye, doubt it not.
    Thy husband too shall think of thee!
By neither shalt thou be forgot,
    Thou *false* to him, thou *fiend* to me!

           *Remember Thee! Remember Thee!*
           Lord Byron

*This last poem was dedicated by Byron to Lady Caroline Lamb. The 'him' referred to in the final line is her cuckolded husband, Lord Melbourne – who, where marriage was concerned, was a sort of Pierre Trudeau of the 19th century.*

# Loss

Having been betrayed, one then has to cope with the agony of loss. How often have I sat shivering in a cooling bath, churning with hatred and misery, writing last letters of renunciation in my head. Invariably included in the letter was the following poem by A. E. Housman, in which I changed the 'she' in line five of the first verse to 'he'. I once copied out the whole poem to send to some erring lover on a piece of Basildon Bond. My parents found it, and got frightfully excited because they assumed I'd written it myself, and they'd produced a genius after all:

Tell me not here, it needs not saying
    What tune the enchantress plays
In aftermaths of soft September
    Or under blanching mays,
For she and I were long acquainted
    And I knew all her ways.

On russet floors, by waters idle,
    The pine lets fall its cone;
The cuckoo shouts all day at nothing
    In leafy dells alone;
And traveller's joy beguiles in autumn
    Hearts that have lost their own.

On acres of the seeded grasses
    The changing burnish heaves;
Or marshalled under moons of harvest
    Stand still all night the sheaves;
Or beeches strip in storms for winter
    And strain the wind with leaves.

Possess, as I possessed a season,
   The countries I resign,
Where over elmy plains the highway
   Would mount the hills and shine,
And full of shade the pillared forest
   Would murmur and be mine.

For nature, heartless, witless nature,
   Will neither care nor know
What stranger's feet may find the meadow
   And trespass there and go,
Nor ask amid the dews of morning
   If they are mine or no.

A. E. Housman

*Now three more poems describing the misery when love is gone.
The first by Tennyson complains that everywhere you go you
are reminded of the loved one. In the second A. E. Housman
claims that this ill-fated love will last for ever. Swinburne, on
the other hand, is more sceptical about such protestations.*

Dark house, by which once more I stand
   Here in the long unlovely street,
   Doors, where my heart was used to beat
So quickly, waiting for a hand.

A hand that can be clasp'd no more –
   Behold me, for I cannot sleep,
   And like a guilty thing I creep
At earliest morning to the door.

He is not here; but far away
   The noise of life begins again,
   And ghastly thro' the drizzling rain
On the bald street breaks the blank day.

from *In Memoriam*,
Alfred, Lord Tennyson

I promise nothing: friends will part;
　All things may end, for all began;
And truth and singleness of heart
　Are mortal even as is man.

But this unlucky love should last
　When answered passions thin to air;
Eternal fate so deep has cast
　Its sure foundation of despair.

　　　　　　　　　　A. E. Housman

I remember the way we parted,
　The day and the way we met;
You hoped we were both broken-hearted,
　And knew we should both forget.

And the best and the worst of this is
　That neither is most to blame,
If you have forgotten my kisses,
　And I have forgotten your name.

*An Interlude*, Algernon Charles Swinburne

*Rupert Brooke has an even more realistic approach. One girl has given him a hard time, so rather heartily he sets out on a walking tour, and vows rather half-heartedly to find another one who won't put him on the rack. Leigh Hunt tries the same strategy.*

Your hands, my dear, adorable,
　Your lips of tenderness
— Oh, I've loved you faithfully and well,
　Three years, or a bit less.
　It wasn't a success.

Thank God, that's done! and I'll take the road,
　Quit of my youth and you,
The Roman road to Wendover
　By Tring and Lilley Hoo,
　As a free man may do.

What's left behind I shall not find,
   The splendour and the pain;
The splash of sun, the shouting wind,
   And the brave sting of rain,
   I may not meet again.

. . . .

And I shall find some girl perhaps,
   And a better one than you,
With eyes as wise, but kindlier,
   And lips as soft, but true,
   And I daresay she will do.

from *The Chilterns*,
Rupert Brooke

'Tis done; I yield; adieu, thou cruel fair!
   Adieu, the averted face, the ungracious cheek!
I go to die, to finish all my care,
   To hang – To hang? – Yes, – round another's neck.

*A Wise Death*, Leigh Hunt

*Perhaps the saddest feeling of all, though, is when we lose someone because we treated them badly, and only discover when they've finally got fed up and pushed off how much we loved them:*

You must live through the time when everything hurts
When the space of the ripe, loaded afternoon
Expands to a landscape of white heat frozen
And trees are weighed down with hearts of stone
And green stares back where you stare alone,
And the walking eyes throw flinty comments
And the words which carry most knives are the blind
Phrases searching to be kind.

Solid and usual objects are ghosts
The furniture carries cargoes of memory,
The staircase has corners which remember

As fire blows red in gusty embers,
And each empty dress cuts out an image
In fur and evening and summer and spring
Of her who was different in each.

Pull down the blind and lie on the bed
And clasp the hour in the glass of one room
Against your mouth like a crystal doom.
Take up the book and stare at the letters
Hieroglyphs on sand and as meaningless –
Here birds crossed once and a foot once trod
In a mist where sight and sound are blurred.

The story of others who made mistakes
And of one whose happiness pierced like a star
Eludes and evades between sentences
And the letters break into eyes which read
The story life writes now in your head,
As though the characters sought for some clue
To their being transcendently living and dead
In your history, worse than theirs, but true.

Set in the mind of their poet, they compare
Their tragic sublime with your tawdry despair
And they have fingers which accuse
You of the double way of shame.
At first you did not love enough
And afterwards you loved too much
And you lacked the confidence to choose
And you have only yourself to blame.

*The Double Shame*, Stephen Spender

## Proposals and Engagements

Love poetry tends to deal with extremes of happiness and despair. The poems quoted in the last section were pretty despairing and tearful, because they comforted me and mirrored my feelings, when I was passing through those restless, feverish, not very happy years, after I'd fled the parental nest, and was searching for a husband to look after me.

I am convinced, however, that some guardian angel was watching over me during those years, not only steering me away from undesirable men, but also keeping me and Leo, my future husband, apart until he was safely separated from his first wife. We had both been brought up in the West Riding together and went to the same children's parties and teenage dances. He remembers being made to eat a huge high tea before coming to one of our dances, in case (horrors) there was cider to drink. We even wrote to each other at school, long letters ending with 'All my love, I must go to choir practice'. I used to douse my letters with Bourjois' Evening in Paris. To this day I have a Valentine card he sent me when I was fourteen. It is covered with roses and bloody hearts. Inside he had written just the words: 'Isn't this awful'.

Well, he went off to fight the Mau Mau in Africa like Lovelace, and when I was eighteen I heard on the grapevine that he was back in England and was getting married. All I thought was, 'How stupid to get married so young'. That year my family moved South and we stayed in a flat in Earl's Court. Unknown to me, Leo and his first wife were living only 50 yards away in another flat. If we had bumped into each other, I should probably have become a friend of both of them, and baby-sat and fed their cats when they were away, and we would never have got off the ground.

Four years later when his marriage was into injury time, I was shopping in Fenwick's, and I saw him and his wife. She was trying on hats. He looked bad-tempered and bored. I was too shy to go and say hello.

But about a year later, when I was just twenty-four, and in despair at ever finding the right person, I went to a pub with my current boyfriend, some insurance broker with whom I was getting on disastrously. During the evening I started talking to a man in spectacles. He said he shared a flat in Chelsea with a man who was recently separated from his wife and who kept lots of cats. He asked me to dine at the flat the following evening. The flat-mate turned out to be Leo. He attacked me with characteristic Yorkshire bluntness all evening. Then, just as I was about to stalk out, he sidled up to me on the sofa, and asked me to have dinner with him in two days' time, on a Wednesday. On the Wednesday morning, I got a letter from him saying how marvellous it was that we should have met up again, and that he couldn't wait to see me in the evening. He ended by quoting two fragments from Donne:

> I am two fools, I know,
> For loving, and for saying so
> In whining Poetry.
>
> I scarce believe my love to be so pure
> As I had thought it was,
> Because it doth endure,
> Vicissitude and season, as the grass.

I was enchanted. Insurance brokers didn't commit themselves like that. For me it was the Cooper de Foudre.

In the evening we went to see Albert Finney in Billy Liar, had dinner and walked home to my flat in Westminster past Hatchard's, where we saw the owner, Sir William Collins, looking at his own books in the window. On the way we picked some daffodils from someone's garden, and I posted them through a pillar box in Birdcage Walk.

For a job, at the time, I was flogging candelabra at the Ideal

Home Exhibition. After meeting Leo, I became so dreamy and disorganized that one morning the Major I was working for suggested I put my hair up to look more efficient. That evening I was meeting Leo for our third date. After dinner he took me back to his flat and removed all the pins from my hair, so it cascaded down like a Galsworthy heroine. Then he said I was never to put it up again because he had decided he wanted to marry me.

Others must have noticed my infatuation. The next day I came across a scrawled half-finished letter one of my flat-mates was writing to the third who was abroad. Seeing my name, I naturally read on:

'Jilly has got a new man,' it said. 'Very nice for a change – it looks as though we're going to have to look for a new flat-mate – quelle drag.'

My husband first brought up the subject of marriage when he was taking my hair down, but perhaps the thought had been forming in his mind for a day or two. One of the lovers' favourite games is asking: when did you really decide? In this extract from Pride and Prejudice, Elizabeth has just got engaged to Mr Darcy:

Elizabeth's spirits soon rising to playfulness again, she wanted Mr Darcy to account for his having ever fallen in love with her.

'How could you begin?' said she. 'I can comprehend your going on charmingly, when you had once made a beginning; but what could set you off in the first place?'

'I cannot fix on the hour, or the spot, or the look, or the words, which laid the foundation. It is too long ago. I was in the middle before I knew that I had begun.'

One of the great running arguments between husband and wife is who actually did the original proposing. Most people drift into a mutual agreement, almost without realizing it – like Miss Hunter Dunn and her Subaltern.

Miss J. Hunter Dunn, Miss J. Hunter Dunn,
Furnish'd and burnish'd by Aldershot sun,
What strenuous singles we played after tea,
We in the tournament – you against me!

Love-thirty, love-forty, oh! weakness of joy,
The speed of a swallow, the grace of a boy,
With carefullest carelessness, gaily you won,
I am weak from your loveliness, Joan Hunter Dunn.

Miss Joan Hunter Dunn, Miss Joan Hunter Dunn,
How mad I am, sad I am, glad that you won.
The warm-handled racket is back in its press,
But my shock-headed victor, she loves me no less.

Her father's euonymus shines as we walk,
And swing past the summer-house, buried in talk,
And cool the verandah that welcomes us in
To the six-o'clock news and a lime-juice and gin.

The scent of the conifers, sound of the bath,
The view from my bedroom of moss-dappled path,
As I struggle with double-end evening tie,
For we dance at the Golf Club, my victor and I.

On the floor of her bedroom lie blazer and shorts
 And the cream-coloured walls are be-trophied with sports,
And westering, questioning settles the sun
On your low-leaded window, Miss Joan Hunter Dunn.

The Hillman is waiting, the light's in the hall,
The pictures of Egypt are bright on the wall,
My sweet, I am standing beside the oak stair
And there on the landing's the light on your hair.

By roads 'not adopted', by woodlanded ways,
She drove to the club in the late summer haze,
Into nine-o'clock Camberley, heavy with bells
And mushroomy, pine-woody, evergreen smells.

Miss Joan Hunter Dunn, Miss Joan Hunter Dunn,
I can hear from the car park the dance has begun.
Oh! full Surrey twilight! importunate band!
Oh! strongly adorable tennis-girl's hand!

Around us are Rovers and Austins afar,
Above us, the intimate roof of the car,
And here on my right is the girl of my choice,
With the tilt of her nose and the chime of her voice.

And the scent of her wrap, and the words never said,
And the ominous, ominous dancing ahead.
We sat in the car park till twenty to one
And now I'm engaged to Miss Joan Hunter Dunn.

*A Subaltern's Love Song*, John Betjeman

*Confined to an all-male society at boarding school, it is hardly surprising that the British male's first love is often for someone of his own sex. The captain of the rugger fifteen, perhaps, or some angelic-faced new boy. Our erotic tastes are often conditioned by our first loves, which probably explains why British men are so frequently drawn to tomboyish girls, jolly good sorts more like chaps. Miss Joan Hunter Dunn, with the 'speed of a swallow, the grace of a boy,' fitted the bill perfectly. Tristram Shandy's Uncle Toby was so shy he never looked at girls at all. His heart in fact was won by the first woman who actually forced him to gaze into her eyes:*

I am half distracted, captain Shandy, said Mrs Wadman, holding up her cambrick handkerchief to her left eye, as she approach'd the door of my uncle Toby's sentry-box – a mote – or sand – or something – I know not what, has got into this eye of mine – do look into it – it is not in the white –

In saying which, Mrs Wadman edged herself close in beside my uncle Toby, and squeezing herself down upon the corner of his bench, she gave him an opportunity of doing it without rising up – Do look into it – she said.

Honest soul! thou didst look into it with as much innocency of heart, as ever child look'd into a raree-shew-box; and 'twere as much a sin to have hurt thee.

If a man will be peeping of his own accord into things of that nature – I've nothing to say to it –

My uncle Toby never did: and I will answer for him, that he would have sat quietly upon a sofa from June to January (which, you know, takes in both the hot and cold months), with an eye as fine as the Thracian Rodope's beside him, without being able to tell, whether it was a black or a blue one.

The difficulty was to get my uncle Toby to look at one at all.

'Tis surmounted. And.

I see him yonder with his pipe pendulous in his hand, and the ashes falling out of it – looking – and looking – then rubbing his eyes – and looking again, with twice the good-nature that ever Gallileo look'd for a spot in the sun.

. . . .

I protest Madame, said my uncle Toby, I see nothing whatever in your eye.

It is not in the white; said Mrs Wadman: my uncle Toby look'd with might and main into the pupil –

Now of all the eyes which ever were created – from your own, Madam, up to those of Venus herself, which certainly were as venereal a pair of eyes as ever stood in a head – there never was an eye of them all, so fitted to rob my uncle Toby of his repose, as the very eye, at which he was looking – it was not, Madam, a rolling eye – a romping or a wanton one – nor was it an eye sparkling – petulant or imperious – of high claims and terrifying exactions, which would have curdled at once that milk of human nature, of which my uncle Toby was made up – but 'twas an eye full of gentle salutations – and soft responses – speaking – not like the trumpet stop of some ill-made organ, in which many an eye I talk to, holds coarse converse – but whispering soft – like the last low accents of an expiring saint – 'How can you love comfortless, captain Shandy, and alone, without a bosom to lean your head on – or trust your cares to?'

It was an eye –
But I shall be in love with it myself, if I say another word about it.

It did my uncle Toby's business.

from Tristram Shandy, Laurence Sterne

*On the eve of Waterloo, Byron wrote:*

> There was a sound of revelry by night,
>     And Belgium's capital had gather'd then
> Her beauty and her chivalry, and bright
>     The lamps shone o'er fair women and brave men.

*One notices the emphasis on* fair *women and* brave *men. For while women are often loved for their beauty, they tend to love men for their courage or their brains. Desdemona, for example, fell in love with Othello for the hardships and adventures he had undergone in battle:*

> Her father lov'd me; oft invited me;
> Still question'd me the story of my life,
> From year to year, the battles, sieges, fortunes
> That I have pass'd.
> I ran it through, even from my boyish days
> To the very moment that he bade me tell it;
> Wherein I spake of most disastrous chances,
> Of moving accidents by flood and field,
> Of hair-breadth 'scapes i' the imminent deadly breach,
> Of being taken by the insolent foe,
> And sold to slavery; of my redemption thence
> And portance in my travel's history;
> Wherein of antres vast and desarts idle,
> Rough quarries, rock and hills whose heads touch heaven,
> It was my hint to speak, such was the process;
> And of the Cannibals that each other eat,
> And Anthropophagi, and men whose heads
> Do grow beneath their shoulders. This to hear

Would Desdemona seriously incline:
But still the house-affairs would draw her thence;
Which ever as she could with haste dispatch,
She'd come again, and with a greedy ear
Devour up my discourse. Which I observing,
Took once a pliant hour, and found good means
To draw from her a prayer of earnest heart
That I would all my pilgrimage dilate,
Whereof by parcels she had something heard,
But not intentively: I did consent;
And often did beguile her of her tears,
When I did speak of some distressful stroke
That my youth suffer'd. My story being done,
She gave me for my pains a world of sighs:
She swore, in faith, 'twas strange, 'twas passing strange;
'Twas pitiful, 'twas wondrous pitiful:
She wish'd she had not heard it; yet she wish'd
That heaven had made her such a man: she thank'd me;
And bade me, if I had a friend that lov'd her,
I should but teach him how to tell my story,
And that would woo her. Upon this hint I spake:
She lov'd me for the dangers I had pass'd,
And I lov'd her that she did pity them.
This only is the witchcraft I have us'd.

from *Othello*, William Shakespeare

*Two more proposals now, the first highly romantic from Daisy
Ashford, the second from Saki, utterly prosaic and quite rightly
turned down:*

She looked very beautiful with some red roses in her hat
and the dainty red ruge in her cheeks looked quite the thing.
Bernard heaved a sigh and his eyes flashed as he beheld her
and Ethel thorght to herself what a fine type of manhood he
reprisented with his nice thin legs in a pale broun trousers and
well fitting spats and a red rose in his button hole and rarther a
sporting cap which gave him a great air with its quaint check

and little flaps to pull down if necessary. Off they started the
envy of all the waiters.

They arrived at Windsor very hot from the jorney and
Bernard at once hired a boat to row his beloved up the river.
Ethel could not row but she much enjoyed seeing the tough
sunburnt arms of Bernard tugging at the oars as she lay among
the rich cushons of the dainty boat. She had a rarther lazy
nature but Bernard did not know of this. However he soon
got dog tired and sugested lunch by the mossy bank.

O yes said Ethel quickly opening the sparkling champagne.

Don't spill any cried Bernard as he carved some chicken.

They eat and drank deeply of the charming viands ending
up with merangs and chocolates.

Let us now bask under the spreading trees said Bernard in a
passiunate tone.

Oh yes lets said Ethel and she opened her dainty parasole
and sank down upon the long green grass. She closed her eyes
but she was far from sleep. Bernard sat beside her in profound
silence gazing at her pink face and long wavy eye lashes. He
puffed at his pipe for some moments while the larks gaily
caroled in the blue sky. Then he edged a trifle closer to Ethels
form.

Ethel he murmered in a trembly voice.

Oh what is it said Ethel hastily sitting up.

Words fail me ejaculated Bernard horsly my passion for you
is intense he added fervently. It has grown day and night since
I first beheld you.

Oh said Ethel in supprise as I am not prepared for this and
she lent back against the trunk of the tree.

Bernard placed one arm tightly round her. When will you
marry me Ethel he uttered you must be my wife it has come
to that I love you so intensely that if you say no I shall perforce
dash my body to the brink of yon muddy river he panted
wildly.

O don't do that implored Ethel breathing rarther hard.

Then say you love me he cried.

Oh Bernard she sighed fervently I certainly love you madly

you are to me like a Heathen god she cried looking at his manly form and handsome flashing face I will indeed marry you.

How soon gasped Bernard gazing at her intensely.

As soon as possible said Ethel gently closing her eyes.

My Darling whispered Bernard and he seized her in his arms we will be married next week.

Oh Bernard muttered Ethel this is so sudden.

*The Young Visiters*, Daisy Ashford

*René:* Well, be patient for a moment, I'm going to say something quite personal and interesting. Will you marry me? The question is sudden, I admit, but these things are best done suddenly. I suppose it was the mention of your great-aunt that suggested it.

*Clare:* The answer is equally sudden. It's 'no.'

*René:* Are you quite sure you mean that?

*Clare:* Convinced.

*René:* How thoroughly sensible of you. So many girls in your place would have said 'Yes.'

*Clare:* I dare say. Our sex hasn't much reputation for discrimination. I didn't know that marrying was in your line.

*René:* It isn't. I dislike the idea of wives about a house: they accumulate dust. Besides, so few of the really nice ones in my set could afford to marry me.

Saki

*Saki's René was on the lookout for a rich wife. But most men find it difficult to propose to a girl who is much better off than they are. Will Ladislaw in* Middlemarch *had the added problem that if he married Dorothea, the girl he loved, she had to forfeit all her fortune. Her first husband was a rich but revolting old prune of a clergyman and also Ladislaw's uncle. Suspecting that Dorothea preferred his handsome nephew, he changed his will before he died, so that Dorothea would be left penniless if she married Ladislaw. Nevertheless, in the end, Dorothea and Ladislaw meet again in what must be one of the most romantic reunions in all literature:*

'Mr Ladislaw,' continued the timid little woman. 'He fears he has offended you, and has begged me to ask if you will see him for a few minutes.'

Dorothea did not answer on the instant: it was crossing her mind that she could not receive him in this library, where her husband's prohibition seemed to dwell. She looked towards the window. Could she go out and meet him in the grounds? The sky was heavy, and the trees had begun to shiver as at a coming storm. Besides, she shrank from going out to him.

'Do see him, Mrs Casaubon,' said Miss Noble, pathetically: 'else I must go back and say No, and that will hurt him.'

'Yes, I will see him,' said Dorothea. 'Pray tell him to come.'

What else was there to be done? There was nothing that she longed for at that moment except to see Will: the possibility of seeing him had thrust itself insistently between her and every other object; and yet she had a throbbing excitement like an alarm upon her – a sense that she was doing something daringly defiant for his sake. . .

'If I love him too much it is because he has been so ill:' – there was a voice within her saying this to some imagined audience in the library, when the door was opened, and she saw Will before her.

She did not move, and he came towards her with more doubt and timidity in his face than she had ever seen before. He was in a state of uncertainty which made him afraid lest some look or word of his should condemn him to a new distance from her; and Dorothea was afraid of her own emotion. She looked as if there were a spell upon her, keeping her motionless and hindering her from unclasping her hands, while some intense, grave yearning was imprisoned within her eyes. Seeing that she did not put out her hand as usual, Will paused a yard from her and said with embarrassment, 'I am so grateful to you for seeing me.'

'I wanted to see you,' said Dorothea, having no other words at command. It did not occur to her to sit down, and Will did not give a cheerful interpretation to this queenly way of receiving him; but he went on to say what he had made up his mind to say.

'I fear you think me foolish and perhaps wrong for coming back so soon. I have been punished for my impatience. You know – every one knows now – a painful story about my parentage. I knew of it before I went away, and I always meant to tell you of it if – if we ever met again.' ...

'You acted as I should have expected you to act,' said Dorothea ...

'I did not believe that you would let any circumstance of my birth create a prejudice in you against me, though it was sure to do so in others,' said Will, shaking his head backward in his old way, and looking with a grave appeal into her eyes.

'If it were a new hardship it would be a new reason for me to cling to you,' said Dorothea, fervidly. 'Nothing could have changed me but –' her heart was swelling, and it was difficult to go on; she made a great effort over herself to say in a low tremulous voice, 'but thinking that you were different – not so good as I had believed you to be.'

'You are sure to believe me better than I am in everything but one,' said Will, giving way to his own feeling in the evidence of hers. 'I mean, in my truth to you. When I thought you doubted of that, I didn't care about anything that was left. I thought it was all over with me, and there was nothing to try for – only things to endure.'

'I don't doubt you any longer,' said Dorothea, putting out her hand; a vague fear for him impelling her unutterable affection.

He took her hand and raised it to his lips with something like a sob. But he stood with his hat and gloves in the other hand, and might have done for the portrait of a Royalist. Still it was difficult to loose the hand, and Dorothea, withdrawing it in a confusion that distressed her, looked and moved away.

'See how dark the clouds have become, and how the trees are tossed,' she said, walking towards the window, yet speaking and moving with only a dim sense of what she was doing.

Will followed her at a little distance, and leaned against the back of a leather chair, on which he ventured now to lay his hat and gloves, and free himself from the intolerable durance of formality to which he had been for the first time condemned in Dorothea's presence. It must be confessed that he felt very happy at that moment leaning on the chair. He was not much afraid of anything that she might feel now.

They stood silent, not looking at each other, but looking at the evergreens which were being tossed, and were showing the pale underside of their leaves against the blackening sky. Will never enjoyed the prospect of a storm so much: it delivered him from the necessity of going away. Leaves and little branches were hurled about, and the thunder was getting nearer. The light was more and more sombre, but there came a flash of lightning which made them start and look at each other, and then smile. Dorothea began to say what she had been thinking of.

'That was a wrong thing for you to say, that you would have had nothing to try for. If we had lost our own chief good, other people's good would remain, and that is worth trying for. Some can be happy. I seemed to see that more clearly than ever, when I was the most wretched. I can hardly think how I could have borne the trouble, if that feeling had not come to me to make strength.'

'You have never felt the sort of misery I felt,' said Will; 'the misery of knowing that you must despise me.'

'But I have felt worse – it was worse to think ill –' Dorothea had begun impetuously, but broke off.

Will coloured. He had the sense that whatever she said was uttered in the vision of a fatality that kept them apart. He was silent a moment, and then said passionately –

'We may at least have the comfort of speaking to each other without disguise. Since I must go away – since we must always be divided – you may think of me as one on the brink of the grave.'

While he was speaking there came a vivid flash of lightning which lit each of them up for the other – and the light seemed to be the terror of a hopeless love. Dorothea darted instantaneously from the window; Will followed her, seizing her hand with a spasmodic movement; and so they stood, with their hands clasped, like two children, looking out on the storm, while the thunder gave a tremendous crack and roll above them, and the rain began to pour down. Then they turned their faces towards each other, with the memory of his last words in them, and they did not loose each other's hand.

'There is no hope for me,' said Will. 'Even if you loved me as well as I love you – even if I were everything to you – I shall most likely always be very poor: on a sober calculation, one can count on nothing but a creeping lot. It is impossible for us ever to belong to each other. It is perhaps base of me to have asked for a word from you. I meant to go away into silence, but I have not been able to do what I meant.'

'Don't be sorry,' said Dorothea, in her clear tender tones. 'I would rather share all the trouble of our parting.'

Her lips trembled, and so did his. It was never known which lips were the first to move towards the other lips; but they kissed tremblingly, and then they moved apart.

The rain was dashing against the window-panes as if an angry spirit were within it, and behind it was the great swoop of the wind; it was one of those moments in which both the busy and the idle pause with a certain awe.

Dorothea sat down on the seat nearest to her, a long low ottoman in the middle of the room, and with her hands folded over each other on her lap, looked at the drear outer world. Will stood still an instant looking at her, then seated himself beside her, and laid his hand on hers, which turned itself upward to be clasped. They sat in that way without looking at each other, until the rain abated and began to fall in stillness. Each had been full of thoughts which neither of them could begin to utter.

But when the rain was quiet, Dorothea turned to look at Will. With passionate exclamation, as if some torture-screw were threatening him, he started up and said, 'It is impossible!'

He went and leaned on the back of the chair again, and

seemed to be battling with his own anger, while she looked towards him sadly.

'It is as fatal as a murder or any other horror that divides people,' he burst out again; 'it is more intolerable – to have our life maimed by petty accidents.'

'No – don't say that – your life need not be maimed,' said Dorothea, gently.

'Yes, it must,' said Will, angrily. 'It is cruel of you to speak in that way – as if there were any comfort. You may see beyond the misery of it, but I don't. It is unkind – it is throwing back my love for you as if it were a trifle, to speak in that way in the face of the fact. We can never be married.'

'Some time – we might,' said Dorothea, in a trembling voice.

'When?' said Will, bitterly. 'What is the use of counting on any success of mine? It is a mere toss up whether I shall ever do more than keep myself decently, unless I choose to sell myself as a mere pen and a mouth-piece. I can see that clearly enough. I could not offer myself to any woman, even if she had no luxuries to renounce.'

There was silence. Dorothea's heart was full of something that she wanted to say, and yet the words were too difficult. She was wholly possessed by them: at that moment debate was mute within her. And it was very hard that she could not say what she wanted to say. Will was looking out of the window angrily. If he would have looked at her and not gone away from her side, she thought everything would have been easier. At last he turned, still resting against the chair, and stretching his hand automatically towards his hat, said with a sort of exasperation, 'Good-bye.'

'Oh, I cannot bear it – my heart will break,' said Dorothea, starting from her seat, the flood of her young passion bearing down all the obstructions which had kept her silent – the great tears rising and falling in an instant: 'I don't mind about poverty – I hate my wealth.'

In an instant Will was close to her and had his arms round her, but she drew her head back and held his away gently that she might go on speaking, her large tear-filled eyes looking at his very simply, while she said in a sobbing childlike way, 'We could live quite well on my own fortune – it is too much – seven hundred a year – I want so little – no new clothes – and I will learn what everything costs.'

from *Middlemarch*, George Eliot

*Dorothea was all openness and lack of guile. By contrast we now see poor Mr Polly being manoeuvred into a joyless marriage by the designing Miriam:*

He put an arm over the back of the seat, and assumed a more comfortable attitude. He glanced at Miriam, who was sitting in a lax, thoughtful pose, with her eyes on the flowers. She was wearing her old dress. She had not had time to change, and the blue tones of her old dress brought out a certain warmth in her skin, and her pose exaggerated whatever was feminine in her rather lean and insufficient body, and rounded her flat chest delusively. A little line of light lay across her profile. The afternoon was full of transfiguring sunshine, children were playing noisily in the adjacent sand-pit, some Judas trees were abloom in the villa gardens that bordered the re-creation ground, and all the place was bright with touches of young summer colour. It all merged with the effect of Miriam in Mr Polly's mind.

Her thought found speech. 'One did ought to be happy in a shop,' she said, with a note of unusual softness in her voice.

It seemed to him that she was right. One did ought to be happy in a shop . . .

'A shop's such a respectable thing to be,' said Miriam thoughtfully.

'*I* could be happy in a shop,' he said.

His sense of effect had made him pause.

'If I had the right company,' he added.

She became very still.

Mr Polly swerved a little from the conversational ice-run upon which he had embarked.

'I'm not such a blooming Geezer,' he said, 'as not to be able to sell goods a bit. One has to be nosy over one's buying, of course. But I shall do all right.'

He stopped, and felt falling, falling through the aching silence that followed.

'If you get the right company,' said Miriam.

'I shall get that all right.'

'You don't mean you've got some one –?'

He found himself plunging.

'I've got some one in my eye this minute,' he said.

'Elfrid!' she said, turning to him. 'You don't mean –'

Well, *did* he mean. 'I do!' he said.

'Not reely!' She clenched her hands to keep still.

He took the conclusive step.

'Well, you and me, Miriam, in a little shop, with a cat and a canary –' He tried too late to get back to a hypothetical note. 'Just suppose it!'

'You mean,' said Miriam, 'You're in love with me, Elfrid?'

What possible answer can a man give to such a question but 'Yes!'

Regardless of the public park, the children in the sandpit, and every one, she bent forward and seized his shoulder and kissed him on the lips. Something lit up in Mr Polly at the touch. He put an arm about her and kissed her back, and felt an irrevocable act was sealed. He had a curious feeling that it would be very satisfying to marry and have a wife – only somehow he wished it wasn't Miriam. Her lips were very pleasant to him, and the feel of her in his arm.

They recoiled a little from each other, and sat for a moment flushed and awkwardly silent. His mind was altogether incapable of controlling its confusion.

'I didn't dream,' said Miriam, 'you cared – Sometimes I thought it was Annie, sometimes Minnie –'

'Always I liked you better than them,' said Mr Polly.

'I love you, Elfrid,' said Miriam, 'since ever we met at your poor father's funeral. Leastways I *would* have done if I had thought – You didn't seem to mean anything you said.'

'I can't believe it!' she added.

'Nor I,' said Mr Polly.

'You mean to marry me and start that little shop?'

'Soon as ever I find it,' said Mr Polly.

'I had no more idea when I came out with you —'

'Nor me.'

'It's like a dream.'

They said no more for a little while.

'I got to pinch myself to think it's real,' said Miriam. 'What they'll do without me at 'ome I can't imagine. When I tell them —'

For the life of him Mr Polly could not tell whether he was fullest of tender anticipations or regretful panic.

'Mother's no good at managing — not a bit. Annie don't care for housework, and Minnie's got no 'ead for it. What they'll do without me I can't imagine.'

'They'll have to do without you,' said Mr Polly, sticking to his guns.

A clock in the town began striking.

'Lor!' said Miriam, 'we shall miss Annie, sitting 'ere and love-making.'

She rose and made as if to take Mr Polly's arm. But Mr Polly felt that their condition must be nakedly exposed to the ridicule of the world by such a linking, and evaded her movement.

Annie was already in sight before a flood of hesitation and terrors assailed Mr Polly.

'Don't tell any one yet a bit,' he said.

'Only Mother,' said Miriam firmly.

from *The History of Mr Polly*, H. G. Wells

*With those words, 'Only Mother', Mr Polly's doom was sealed.*

# The Parental Boot

*Once parents know an engagement is in the air, it is very difficult for a young man to back out. Mrs Bennet, having cordially detested Mr Darcy for his arrogance, displays a staggering volte face when she suddenly learns he wants to marry one of her daughters. Lady Bracknell is much more exacting when Jack Worthing asks for the hand of her daughter Gwendolen.*

When her mother went up to her dressing-room at night she [Elizabeth] followed her, and made the important communication. Its effect was most extraordinary; for, on first hearing it, Mrs Bennet sat quite still, and unable to utter a syllable. Nor was it under many, many minutes, that she could comprehend what she heard, though not in general backward to credit what was for the advantage of her family, or that came in the shape of a lover to any of them. She began at length to recover, to fidget about in her chair, get up, sit down again, wonder, and bless herself.

'Good gracious! Lord bless me! only think! dear me! Mr Darcy! Who would have thought it? And is it really true? Oh, my sweetest Lizzy! how rich and how great you will be! What pin-money, what jewels, what carriages you will have! Jane's is nothing to it – nothing at all. I am so pleased – so happy! Such a charming man! – so handsome! so tall! Oh my dear Lizzy! pray apologize for my having disliked him so much before. I hope he will overlook it. Dear, dear Lizzy. A house in town! Everything that is charming! Three daughters married! Ten thousand a year! Oh, Lord! what will become of me. I shall go distracted.'

This was enough to prove that her approbation need not be

doubted; and Elizabeth, rejoicing that such an effusion was heard only by herself, soon went away. But before she had been three minutes in her own room, her mother followed her.

'My dearest child,' she cried, 'I can think of nothing else! Ten thousand a year, and very likely more! 'Tis as good as a lord! And a special license – you must and shall be married by a special license. But, my dearest love, tell me what dish Mr Darcy is particularly fond of, that I may have it to-morrow.'

from *Pride and Prejudice*, Jane Austen

*Lady Bracknell:* I feel bound to tell you that you are not down on my list of eligible young men, although I have the same list as the dear Duchess of Bolton has. We work together, in fact. However, I am quite ready to enter your name, should your answers be what a really affectionate mother requires. Do you smoke?

*Jack:* Well, yes, I must admit I smoke.

*Lady Bracknell:* I am glad to hear it. A man should always have an occupation of some kind. There are far too many idle men in London as it is. How old are you?

*Jack:* Twenty-nine.

*Lady Bracknell:* A very good age to be married at. I have always been of opinion that a man who desires to get married should know either everything or nothing. Which do you know?

*Jack:* I know nothing, Lady Bracknell.

*Lady Bracknell:* I am pleased to hear it. I do not approve of anything that tampers with natural ignorance. Ignorance is like a delicate exotic fruit; touch it and the bloom is gone. The whole theory of Modern education is radically unsound. Fortunately in England, at any rate, education produces no effect whatsoever. If it did, it would prove a serious danger to the upper classes, and probably lead to acts of violence in Grosvenor Square. What is your income?

*Jack:* Between seven and eight thousand a year.

*Lady Bracknell:* In land, or in investments?

*Jack:* In investments, chiefly.

*Lady Bracknell:* That is satisfactory. What between the duties expected of one during one's lifetime, and the duties exacted from one after one's death, land has ceased to be either a profit or a pleasure. It gives one position, and prevents one from keeping it up. That's all that can be said about land.

from *The Importance of Being Earnest*, Oscar Wilde

*Other people go through hordes of boyfriends. My long-suffering parents had to put up with a string of stockbrokers, police constables, ski instructors, American Airforcemen, lay-about journalists and Portuguese fishermen with fading sun tans. They were invariably polite to all of them, because they were never quite sure that 'Old Jilly' wouldn't end up marrying one.*

*Parents, in fact, have to put up with a lot when their children are courting. The Pooters, for example, were given a hard time when their son Lupin fell in love with the fearful Daisy Mutlar:*

November 5 – Sunday.
Carrie and I troubled about that mere boy Lupin, getting engaged to be married without consulting us or anything. After dinner he told us all about it. He said the lady's name was Daisy Mutlar, and she was the nicest, prettiest, and most accomplished girl he ever met. He loved her the moment he saw her, and if he had to wait fifty years he would wait, and he knew she would wait for him. Lupin further said, with much warmth, that the world was a different world to him now – it was a world worth living in. He lived with an object now, and that was to make Daisy Mutlar – Daisy Pooter, and he would guarantee she would not disgrace the family of the Pooters. Carrie here burst out crying, and threw her arms round his neck, and in doing so upset the glass of port he held in his hand all over his new light trousers.

I said I had no doubt we should like Miss Mutlar when we saw her, but Carrie said she loved her already. I thought this rather premature, but held my tongue. Daisy Mutlar was the sole topic of conversation for the remainder of the day. I asked Lupin who her people were, and he replied: 'Oh, you know Mutlar, Williams and Watts.' I did not know, but refrained from asking any further questions at present, for fear of irritating Lupin.

. . . .

*November* 9 – Lupin has Daisy Mutlar on the brain, so we see little of him, except that he invariably turns up at meal times.

. . . .

*November* 15 – Lupin was restless and unbearable till his Daisy Mutlar and Frank arrived.

Carrie and I were rather startled at Daisy's appearance. She had a bright-crimson dress on, cut very low in the neck. I do not think such a style modest. She ought to have taken a lesson from Carrie and covered her shoulders with a little lace.

. . . .

*November* 19 – Sunday.

A delightfully quiet day. In the afternoon Lupin was off to spend the rest of the day with the Mutlars. He departed in the best of spirits, and Carrie said: 'Well, one advantage of Lupin's engagement with Daisy is that the boy seems happy all day long. That quite reconciles me to what I must confess seems an imprudent engagement.'

. . . .

About nine o'clock, to our surprise, Lupin entered, with a wild, reckless look, and in a hollow voice, which I must say seemed rather theatrical, said: 'Have you any brandy?' I said: 'No; but here is some whisky.' Lupin drank off nearly a wineglassful without water, to my horror.

We all three sat reading in silence till ten, when Carrie and I rose to go to bed. Carrie said to Lupin: 'I hope Daisy is well?'

Lupin, with a forced careless air that he must have picked up from the 'Holloway Comedians,' replied: 'Oh, Daisy? You mean Miss Mutlar. I don't know whether she is well or not, but please *never to mention her name again in my presence.*'

*December* 21 ... In the evening Lupin was very low-spirited, and I reminded him that behind the clouds the sun was shining. He said: 'Ugh! it never shines on me.' I said: 'Stop, Lupin, my boy; you are worried about Daisy Mutlar. Don't think of her any more. You ought to congratulate yourself on having got off a very bad bargain. Her notions are far too grand for our simple tastes.'

He jumped up and said: 'I won't allow one word to be uttered against her. She's worth the whole bunch of your friends put together, that inflated sloping-head of a Perkupp included.' I left the room with silent dignity but caught my foot in the mat.

*December 23* – I exchanged no words with Lupin in the morning; but as he seemed to be in exuberant spirits in the evening I ventured to ask him where he intended to spend his Christmas. He replied: 'Oh most likely at the Mutlars.'

In wonderment, I said: 'What! after your engagement has been broken off?'

Lupin said: 'Who said it is off?'

I said: 'You have given us both to understand –'

He interrupted me by saying: 'Well, never mind what I said. *It is on again – there!*'

> from *The Diary of a Nobody*, George & Weedon Grossmith

*Now to a favourite book*, Diary of a Provincial Lady, *where we see that parents sometimes behave even more appallingly than their children. Mrs Blenkinsop's histrionic reaction to her daughter Barbara's engagement soon has a quiet country village revelling in gossip and taking sides:*

*April 2nd* – Sit, seething with excitement, in the hope that I am at least going to be told that Barbara is engaged. Try to keep this out of sight, and to maintain expression of earnest and sympathetic attention only, whilst Barbara says that it is sometimes very difficult to know which way Duty lies, that she has always thought a true woman's highest vocation is home-making, and that the love of a Good Man is the crown of life. I say Yes, Yes, to all of this . . .

Barbara at length admits that Crosbie has asked her to marry him – he did it, she says, at the Zoo – and go out with him as his wife to the Himalayas. This, says Barbara, is where all becomes difficult. She may be old-fashioned – no doubt she is – but can she leave her mother alone? No, she cannot. Can she, on the other hand, give up dear Crosbie, who has never loved a girl before, and says that he never will again? No, she cannot.

Barbara weeps. I kiss her. Howard Fitzsimmons selects this moment to walk in with the tea, at which I sit down again in confusion and begin to talk about the Vicarage daffodils being earlier than ours.

. . . .

*April 4th* – Go to see old Mrs Blenkinsop. She is, as usual, swathed in shawls, but has exchanged *Lord Beaconsfield* for *Froude and Carlyle*. She says that I am very good to come and see a poor old woman, and that she often wonders how it is that so many of the younger generation seem to find their way to her by instinct. Is it, she suggests, because her *heart* has somehow kept young, in spite of her grey hair and wrinkles, ha-ha-ha, and so she has always been able to find the Silver Lining, she is thankful to say. I circuitously approach the topic of Barbara. Mrs B. at once says that the young are very hard and selfish. This is natural, perhaps, but it saddens her. Not on her own account – no, no, no – but because she cannot bear to think of what Barbara will have to suffer from remorse when it is Too Late.

. . . .

I feel that we are getting no further, and boldly introduce the name of Crosbie Carruthers. Terrific effect on Mrs B., who puts her hand on her heart, leans back, and begins to gasp and turn blue. She is sorry, she pants, to be so foolish, but it is now many nights since she has had any sleep at all, and the strain is beginning to tell. I must forgive her. I hastily do forgive her, and depart.

. . . .

*April 10th* – Entire parish now seething with the *affaire* Blen-

kinsop. Old Mrs B. falls ill, and retires to bed. Barbara bicycles
madly up and down between her mother and the garden of the
*Cross and Keys*, where C.C. spends much time reading copies
of *The Times of India* and smoking small cigars. We are all
asked by Barbara What she Ought to Do, and all give different
advice. Deadlock appears to have been reached, when C.C.
suddenly announces that he is summoned to London and must
have an answer One Way or the Other immediately.

Old Mrs B. – who has been getting better and taking Port –
instantly gets worse again and says that she will not stand in
the way of dear Barbara's happiness.

Period of fearful stress sets in, and Barbara and C.C. say
Good-bye in the front sitting-room of the *Cross and Keys*.
They have, says Barbara in tears, parted For Ever, and Life is
Over, and will I take the Guides' Meeting for her tonight –
which I agree to do.

. . . .

*April 12th* – Receive a letter from Mary K. with postscript: Is
it true that Barbara Blenkinsop is engaged to be married? and
am also asked the same question by Lady B., who looks in on
her way to some ducal function on the other side of the
county. Have no time in which to enjoy being in the superior
position of bestowing information, as Lady B. at once adds
that *she* always advises girls to marry, no matter what the man
is like, as any husband is better than none, and there are not
nearly enough to go round.

. . . .

*April 14th* – Cook electrifies me by asking me if I have heard
that Miss Barbara Blenkinsop's engagement is on again, it's all
over the village. The gentleman, she says, came down by the
8.45 last night, and is at the *Cross and Keys*. As it is exactly
9.45 a.m. when she tells me this, I ask how she knows? Cook
merely repeats that It is All Over the Village, and that Miss
Barbara will quite as like as not be married by special licence,
and old Mrs B. is in such a way as never was. Am disconcerted
to find that Cook and I have been talking our heads off for the

better part of forty minutes before I remember that gossip is both undignified and undesirable.

from *Diary of a Provincial Lady*, E. M. Delafield

*Barbara finally married her Crosbie but, with such parents about, it is hardly surprising that some suitors do their best to avoid contact with their future in-laws.*

The hunchèd camels of the night*
Trouble the bright
And silver waters of the moon.
The Maiden of the Morn will soon
Through Heaven stray and sing,
Star gathering.

Now while the dark about our loves is strewn,
Light of my dark, blood of my heart, O come!
And night will catch her breath up, and be dumb.

Leave thy father, leave thy mother
And thy brother;
Leave the black tents of thy tribe apart!
Am I not thy father and thy brother,
And thy mother?
And thou – what needest with thy tribe's black tents
Who hast the red pavilion of my heart?

*Arab Love-Song*, Francis Thompson

* Cloud shapes observed by travellers in the East.

# Weddings

*At last the wedding is in sight. But the bride will be so busy making lists, writing thank-you letters, dragooning bridesmaids into frightful dresses, and going on pre-wedding crash diets, that it's no wonder that on the actual day, she'll be far too exhausted to worry whether her guests are enjoying themselves.*

Well, after about two days they did go, well it seemed like that, and there was all that *plebeian* revelry with *rice* and confetti and old *boots* and everything, my dear *nobody* adores clean fun more than I do, but I do think when a girl's best friends are seeing her off into the New Life which stretches before her and everything they *might* think of something more *affectionate* to do than throw cereals down a girl's *back* don't you? but there it is, that's *weddings* and I suppose it's a kind of unconscious *revenge* for all the *sufferings* of the wedding-guests, well there we were, my dear, *suspended* in mid-air so to speak, at Stoke-under-the-Wallop at half-past-five in the afternoon, all the girls half-dead with ices and standing on one leg and all the men half-alive with champagne and no train till 6.15, and two *Satanical* changes at that, my dear, *too* pulverizing.

from *Weddings*, A. P. Herbert

*The bridegroom, on the other hand, can't wait to escape from the reception to get his bride into bed.*

Ah! when will this long weary day have end,
And lende me leave to come unto my love?
How slowly do the houres they'r numbers spend!
How slowly does sad Time his feathers move!

Hast thee, O fayrest planet, to thy home
Within the westerne fome.
Thy tyred steedes long since have need of rest.
Long though it be, at last I see it gloome,
And the bright evening star with golden creast
Appeare out of the east.
Fayre childe of beauty, glorious lampe of love,
That all the host of heaven in rankes doost lead,
And guydest lovers through the nightes sad dread,
How cheerfully thou lookest from above,
And seemst to laugh atweene thy twinkling light,
As joying in the sight
Of these glad many, which for joy doe sing,
That all the woods them answer, and their echo ring.

from *Epithalamion*, Edmund Spenser

*Occasionally a gate-, or should it be, a drawbridge-crasher,
turns up at the wedding and provides an unexpected cabaret.
Lochinvar must be Walter Scott's greatest romantic hero. He
really proved that love can conquer all:*

O, young Lochinvar is come out of the west,
Through all the wide Border his steed was the best;
And save his good broad-sword he weapons had none,
He rode all unarmed, and he rode all alone,
So faithful in love, and so dauntless in war,
There never was knight like the young Lochinvar.

He staid not for brake, and he stopped not for stone;
He swam the Eske river where ford there was none;
But ere he alighted at Netherby gate,
The bride had consented, the gallant came late:
For a laggard in love, and a dastard in war,
Was to wed the fair Ellen of brave Lochinvar.

So boldly he enter'd the Netherby Hall,
Among bride's-men, the kinsmen, and brothers, and all:
Then spoke the bride's father, his hand on his sword,

(For the poor craven bridegroom said never a word,)
'O come ye in peace here, or come ye in war,
Or to dance at our bridal, young Lord Lochinvar?'

'I long woo'd your daughter, my suit you denied; –
Love swells like the Solway, but ebbs like its tide –
And now am I come, with this lost love of mine,
To lead but one measure, drink one cup of wine.
There are maidens in Scotland more lovely by far,
That would gladly be bride to the young Lochinvar.'

The bride kissed the goblet: the knight took it up,
He quaffed off the wine, and he threw down the cup.
She looked down to blush, and she looked up to sigh,
With a smile on her lips, and a tear in her eye.
He took her soft hand ere her mother could bar, –
'Now tread we a measure!' said young Lochinvar.

So stately his form, and so lovely her face,
That never a hall such a galliard did grace;
While her mother did fret, and her father did fume,
And the bridegroom stood dangling his bonnet and plume;
And the bride-maidens whisper'd, ' 'Twere better by far
To have match'd our fair cousin with young Lochinvar.'

One touch to her hand, and one word in her ear,
When they reach'd the hall-door, and the charger stood near;
So light to the saddle before her he sprung! –
'She is won! we are gone, over bank, bush, and scaur;
They'll have fleet steeds that follow,' quoth young Lochinvar.

There was mounting 'mong Graemes of the Netherby clan;
Forsters, Fenwicks, and Musgraves, they rode and they ran:
There was racing and chasing, on Cannobie Lee,
But the lost bride of Netherby ne'er did they see.
So daring in love, and so dauntless in war,
Have ye ne'er heard of gallant like young Lochinvar?

*Lochinvar*, Sir Walter Scott

# For Better. . .

*A happy marriage is the best thing life has to offer. It is built up brick by brick over the years and cemented as much by the moments of tenderness as by those of irritation.*

*From Bertrand Russell, we now have as good an argument as any for the advantages of a secure and contented relationship:*

Love is something far more than desire for sexual intercourse; it is the principal means of escape from the loneliness which affects most men and women throughout the greater part of their lives. There is a deep-seated fear, in most people, of the cold world and the possible cruelty of the herd; there is a longing for affection, which is often concealed by roughness, boorishness or a bullying manner in men, and by nagging and scolding in women. Passionate mutual love while it lasts puts an end to this feeling; it breaks down the hard walls of the ego, producing a new being composed of two in one. Nature did not construct human beings to stand alone, since they cannot fulfil her biological purpose except with the help of another; and civilized people cannot fully satisfy their sexual instinct without love. The instinct is not completely satisfied unless a man's whole being, mental quite as much as physical, enters into the relation. Those who have never known the deep intimacy and the intense companionship of mutual love have missed the best thing that life has to give; unconsciously, if not consciously, they feel this, and the resulting disappointment inclines them towards envy, oppression and cruelty. To give due place to passionate love should be therefore a matter which concerns the sociologist, since, if they miss this experience, men and women cannot attain their full stature, and cannot feel towards the rest of the world that kind of generous warmth without which their social activities are pretty sure to be harmful.

*Love, An Escape From Loneliness*, Bertrand Russell

*Now — marriage seen by four different authors. Anyone newly married will understand Eve's total dependence on Adam for her happiness. Milton appears to have been a pretty unsatisfactory husband, but here we catch him in a rare moment of tenderness. T. S. Eliot's lovely poem praises the sexual and intellectual compatability he achieved with his second wife. Adrian Mitchell shows how thoughts of the loved one cheer one up in the darkest moments. While Shakespeare argues that the true lover is capable of constancy.*

With thee conversing I forget all time,
All seasons and their change, all please alike.
Sweet is the breath of morn, her rising sweet
With charm of earliest Birds; pleasant the Sun
When first on this delightful Land he spreads
His orient Beams, on herb, tree, fruit and floure,
Glistring with dew; fragrant the fertil earth
After soft showers; and sweet the coming on
Of grateful Evning milde, then silent Night
With this her solemn Bird and this fair Moon,
And these the Gemms of Heav'n, her starrie train:
But neither breath of Morn when she ascends
With charm of earliest Birds, nor rising Sun
On this delightful land, nor herb, fruit, floure,
Glistring with dew, nor fragrance after showers,
Nor grateful Evning mild, nor silent Night
With this her solemn Bird, nor walk by Moon,
Or glittering Starr-light without thee is sweet.

from *Paradise Lost*, John Milton

To whom I owe the leaping delight
That quickens my senses in our wakingtime

And the rhythm that governs the repose of our sleepingtime,
    The breathing in unison

Of lovers whose bodies smell of each other
Who think the same thoughts without need of speech
And babble the same speech without need of meaning.

No peevish winter wind shall chill
No sullen tropic sun shall wither
The roses in the rose-garden which is ours and ours only

But this dedication is for others to read:
These are private words addressed to you in public.

                              *A Dedication to my Wife*, T. S. Eliot

            When I am sad and weary,
            When I think all hope has gone.
            When I walk along High Holborn
            I think of you with nothing on.

                *Celia Celia*, Adrian Mitchell

Let me not to the marriage of true minds
Admit impediments. Love is not love
Which alters when it alteration finds,
Or bends with the remover to remove:
O, no! it is an ever-fixed mark,
That looks on tempests and is never shaken;
It is the star to every wandering bark,
Whose worth's unknown, although his height be taken.
Love's not Time's fool, though rosy lips and cheeks
Within his bending sickle's compass come;
Love alters not with his brief hours and weeks,
But bears it out even to the edge of doom.
    If this be error and upon me proved,
    I never writ, nor no man ever loved.

                *Sonnet CXVI*, William Shakespeare

## For Worse . . .

One of the things that shocked me most during the first year of my marriage was the overwhelming black gloom that used to sweep over me without warning. It made me feel horribly guilty. Here I was, I had achieved my heart's desire – I knew I ought to be happy. I was happy – for a lot of the time. Yet I couldn't reconcile the intense love I felt for my husband with these pulverizing bouts of despair. Marriage is such an adjustment that, in retrospect, I think they were probably caused by exhaustion. What I felt, however, seemed to be summed up by D. H. Lawrence's poem To a Young Wife:

> The pain of loving you
> Is almost more than I can bear.
>
> I walk in fear of you.
> The darkness starts up where
> You stand, and the night comes through
> Your eyes when you look at me.
>
> Ah never before did I see
> The shadows that live in the sun!
>
> Now every tall glad tree
> Turns round its back to the sun
> And looks down on the ground, to see
> The shadow it used to shun.
>
> At the foot of each glowing thing
> A night lies looking up.
>
> Oh, and I want to sing
> And dance, but I can't lift up

My eyes from the shadows: dark
They lie spilt round the cup.

What is it? – Hark
The faint fine seethe in the air!

Like the seething sound in a shell!
It is death still seething where
The wild-flower shakes its bell
And the skylark twinkles blue –

The pain of loving you
Is almost more than I can bear.

*To a Young Wife*, D. H. Lawrence

*Lawrence loved too much, but Edward Thomas, in a beautiful,
wise, amazingly honest poem, confesses he loved too little.
While Coventry Patmore was faced with the problem that,
having married his wife, he still didn't feel she was wholly his.*

No one so much as you
Loves this my clay,
Or would lament as you
Its dying day.

You know me through and through
Though I have not told,
And though with what you know
You are not bold.

None ever was so fair
As I thought you:
Not a word can I bear
Spoken against you.

All that I ever did
For you seemed coarse
Compared with what I hid
Nor put in force.

My eyes scarce dare meet you
Lest they should prove
I but respond to you
And do not love.

We look and understand
We cannot speak
Except in trifles and
Words the most weak.

For I at most accept
Your love, regretting
That is all: I have kept
Only a fretting

That I could not return
All that you gave
And could not ever burn
With the love you have,

Till sometimes it did seem
Better it were
Never to see you more
Than linger here

With only gratitude
Instead of love –
A pine in solitude
Cradling a dove.

*No One So Much as You*,
Edward Thomas

Why, having won her, do I woo?
    Because her spirit's vestal grace
Provokes me always to pursue,
    But, spirit-like, eludes embrace;
Because her womanhood is such

That, as on court-days subjects kiss
The Queen's hand, yet so near a touch
Affirms no mean familiarness.

from *The Married Lover*,
Coventry Patmore

*Many couples row about money, of which there is never enough: 'We possessed all the universe together,' said one of Shaw's characters,*

and you ask me to give you my scanty wages as well. I have given you the greatest of all things; and you ask me to give you little things. I gave you your own soul: you ask for my body as a plaything. Was it not enough? Was it not enough?

*In our house, we row a great deal over the dogs. My husband complains they are quite out of control and that I spoil them impossibly. Mr and Mrs Pepys obviously had the same problem:*

At night my wife and I did fall out about the dog's being put down in the cellar, which I had a mind to have done because of his fouling the house, and I would have my will; and so we went to bed and lay all night in a quarrel.

Samuel Pepys

*Portia, on the other hand, had the complaint of many wives today, that her husband had become totally preoccupied with business, and never shared his worries with her. In this case, the worries were quite considerable. Brutus is plotting to murder Caesar the following day.*

Brutus: Kneel not, gentle Portia.
Portia: I should not need, if you were gentle Brutus.
   Within the bond of marriage, tell me, Brutus,
   Is it excepted I should know no secrets
   That appertain to you? Am I yourself

But, as it were, in sort of limitation –
To keep with you at meals, comfort your bed,
And talk to you sometimes? Dwell I but in the suburbs
Of your good pleasure? If it be no more,
Portia is Brutus' harlot, not his wife.

*Brutus:* You are my true and honourable wife;
As dear to me as are the ruddy drops
That visit my sad heart.

*Portia:* If this were true, then should I know this secret.
I grant I am a woman; but withal
A woman that lord Brutus took to wife:
I grant I am a woman; but withal
A woman well-reputed – Cato's daughter.
Think you I am no stronger than my sex,
Being so fathered and so husbanded?
Tell me your counsels; I will not disclose 'em:
I have made strong proof of my constancy,
Giving myself a voluntary wound
Here, in the thigh. Can I bear that with patience,
And not my husband's secrets?

*Brutus:* O ye gods,
Render me worthy of this noble wife! (*Knocking within*)
Hark! hark! one knocks. Portia, go in awhile;
And by and by thy bosom shall partake
The secrets of my heart.

from Julius Caesar,<br>William Shakespeare

*Finally, the couple in Louis MacNeice's poem found that
marriage never quite came up to their romantic expectations.
I've always been haunted by the lines:*

So they were married – to be the more together –
And found they were never again so much together.

Life in a day: he took his girl to the ballet;
Being shortsighted himself could hardly see it –
  The white skirts in the grey

Glade and the swell of the music
Lifting the white sails.

Calyx upon calyx, canterbury bells in the breeze
The flowers on the left mirror to the flowers on the right
   And the naked arms above
   The powdered faces moving
   Like seawood in a pool.

Now, he thought, we are floating – ageless, oarless –
Now there is no separation, from now on
   You will be wearing white
   Satin and a red sash
   Under the waltzing trees.

But the music stopped, the dancers took their curtain,
The river had come to a lock – a shuffle of programmes –
   And we cannot continue down
   Stream unless we are ready
   To enter the lock and drop.

So they were married – to be the more together –
And found they were never again so much together,
   Divided by the morning tea,
   By the evening paper,
   By the children and tradesmen's bills.

Waking at times in the night she found assurance
In his regular breathing but wondered whether
   It was really worth it and where
   The river had flowed away
   And where were the white flowers.

                     *Les Sylphides*, Louis MacNeice

# How Sad and Mad and Bad It Was —
# But Then, How It Was Sweet

*Another of the great problems of marriage is to prevent it going stale. 'To plod on,' said Meredith, 'and still keep the passion fresh.' Dryden's couple thought the solution was an open marriage. While Kipling's junior officer dreamed up an ingenious scheme to repel all invaders.*

Fair Iris I love, and hourly I dye,
But not for a Lip, nor a languishing Eye:
She's fickle and false, and there we agree;
For I am as false, and as fickle as she:
We neither believe what either can say;
And, neither believing, we neither betray.

'Tis Civil to swear, and say things of course;
We mean not the taking for better for worse.
When present, we love; when absent, agree:
I think not of Iris, nor Iris of me:
The Legend of Love no Couple can find
So easie to part, or so equally join'd.

from *Amphitryon* (Mercury's Song to Phaedra),
John Dryden

Now Jones had left his new-wed bride to keep his house in
    order,
And hied away to the Hurrum Hills above the Afghan border,
To sit on a rock with a heliograph; but ere he left he taught
His wife the working of the Code that sets the miles at naught.

And Love had made him very sage, as Nature made her fair;
So Cupid and Apollo linked, *per* heliograph, the pair.
At dawn, across the Hurrum Hills, he flashed her counsel wise –
At e'en, the dying sunset bore her husband's homilies.

He warned her 'gainst seductive youths in scarlet clad and
  gold,
As much as 'gainst the blandishments paternal of the old;
But kept his gravest warnings for (hereby the ditty hangs)
That snowy-haired Lothario, Lieutenant-General Bangs.

'Twas General Bangs, with Aide and Staff, who tittupped on
  the way,
When they beheld a heliograph tempestuously at play.
They thought of Border risings, and of stations sacked and
  burnt –
So stopped to take the message down – and this is what they
  learnt –
'Dash dot dot, dot, dot dash, dot dash dot,' twice. The General
  swore.
'Was ever General Officer addressed as "dear" before?
' "My Love," i' faith! "My Duck," Gadzooks! "My darling
  popsy-wop!"'
'Spirit of great Lord Wolseley, who is on that mountaintop?'

The artless Aide-de-camp was mute, the gilded Staff were
  still,
As, dumb with pent-up mirth, they booked that message from
  the hill;
For clear as summer lightning-flare, the husband's warning
  ran: –
'Don't dance or ride with General Bangs – a most immoral
  man.'

At dawn, across the Hurrum Hills, he flashed her counsel
  wise –
But, howsoever Love be blind, the world at large hath eyes.

With damnatory dot and dash he heliographed his wife
Some interesting details of the General's private life.

The artless Aide-de-camp was mute, the shining Staff were
still
And red and ever redder grew the General's shaven gill.
And this is what he said at last (his feelings matter not): —
'I think we've tapped a private line. Hi! Threes about there!
Trot!'

All honour unto Bangs, for ne'er did Jones thereafter know
By word or act official who read off that helio.
But the tale is on the Frontier, and from Michni to Mooltan
They know the worthy General as 'that most immoral man.'

*A Code of Morals*, Rudyard Kipling

*Arthur Hugh Clough disapproved of any kind of playing around:*

> Do not adultery commit,
> Advantage rarely comes of it.

*On the other hand, bounders, as Shakespeare points out in*
The Winter's Tale, *take advantage:*

> Many a man there is . . . holds his wife by th'arm
> That little thinks she has been sluiced in his absence
> And his pond fished by his next neighbour,
> By Sir Smile, his neighbour.

*Brilliant that Sir Smile, a sort of wolf in sheep's clothing.*
*Shakespeare obviously felt very strongly about adultery, or he*
*could never have painted Othello's anguish so effectively when*
*he thinks his wife is being unfaithful:*

> O curse of marriage,
> That we can call these delicate creatures ours,
> And not their appetites. I had rather be a toad
> And live upon the vapour of a dungeon,
> Than keep a corner in the thing I love
> For others' uses.

*The only answer, according to John Donne, is for the adulterers to keep their traps shut, and not let anyone find out:*

> So let us melt, and make no noise,
> No tear-floods, nor sigh-tempests move,
> 'Twere profanation of our joys
> To tell the laity our love.

*Women, when they start an affair, improve enormously in looks. Their eyes shine, their coats gleam as though they've just taken a course in Bob Martin's, and they have a bedia-monded look even if they're not wearing any jewellery. One husband said he could always tell when his wife was having an affair, because the poetry books were suddenly at the horizontal on top of the shelves. Like Mariana of the Moated Grange, who hated late afternoon most of all, the unfaithful wife dreads the coming of 5.30, when the danger zone of her husband returning home has been entered, and she knows now it's too late for the lover to telephone.*

> With blackest moss the flower-plots
> Were thickly crusted, one and all:
> The rusted nails fell from the knots
> That held the pear to the gable-wall.
> The broken sheds look'd sad and strange:
> Unlifted was the clinking latch;
> Weeded and worn the ancient thatch
> Upon the lonely moated grange.
> She only said, 'My life is dreary,
> He cometh not,' she said;
> She said, 'I am aweary, aweary,
> I would that I were dead!'
>
> Her tears fell with the dews at even;
> Her tears fell ere the dews were dried;
> She would not look on the sweet heaven,
> Either at morn or eventide.

After the flitting of the bats,
When thickest dark did trance the sky,
She drew her casement-curtain by,
And glanced athwart the glooming flats.
She only said, 'The night is dreary,
He cometh not,' she said:
She said, 'I am aweary, aweary,
I would that I were dead!'

. . . .

The sparrow's chirrup on the roof,
The slow clock ticking, and the sound
Which to the wooing wind aloof
The poplar made, did all confound
Her sense; but most she loathed the hour
When the thick-moted sunbeam lay
Athwart the chambers, and the day
Was sloping toward his western bower.
Then, said she, 'I am very dreary,
He will not come,' she said;
She wept, 'I am aweary, aweary,
Oh God, that I were dead!'

from *Mariana*,
Alfred, Lord Tennyson

*For a respectable Victorian, Tennyson knew a lot about in-*
*fidelity. Few of the discreet family parties, listening to the*
*daughter of the house trilling out 'Come into the Garden,*
*Maud', realized that this was a song about an adulterous affair.*
*The married lover lurked in the summer garden, watching the*
*seventeen-year-old Maud going through her automatic paces on*
*the dance floor, and waiting for her to steal out into the night*
*and snatch a kiss, and goodness knows what else, when no one*
*was looking:*

Come into the garden, Maud,
For the black bat, night, has flown;
Come into the garden, Maud,

I am here at the gate alone;
And the woodbine spices are wafted abroad
And the musk of the rose is blown.

. . . .

The slender acacia would not shake
One long milk-bloom on the tree;
The white lake-blossom fell into the lake,
As the pimpernel dozed on the lea;
But the rose was awake all night for your sake
Knowing your promise to me;
The lilies and roses were all awake,
They sighed for the dawn and thee.

. . . .

There has fallen a splendid tear
From the passion-flower at the gate.
She is coming, my dove, my dear;
She is coming, my life, my fate;
The red rose cries, 'She is near, she is near;'
And the white rose weeps, 'she is late;'
The larkspur listens, 'I hear, I hear;'
And the lily whispers, 'I wait.'

from *Maud*,
Alfred, Lord Tennyson

*'So free we seem, so fettered fast we are,' wrote Browning
wistfully. Convention, in fact, is very strong, and it has to be
a very passionate affair to push a marriage on to the rocks.
Usually the husband or wife finds out, or the whole thing becomes too much of a hassle, so the lovers regretfully decide to
pack it in.*

*Two fragments always come to my mind in this context. The
first, from Oscar Wilde's Ballad of Reading Gaol, seems to sum
up the strain of carrying on an adulterous affair:*

For he who lives more lives than one
More deaths than one must die.

*The second, from A. E. Housman, illustrates the folly of starting an affair that can only end in tears:*

> For the game is ended,
> That should not have begun.

*Both fragments, in fact, applied to the subterfuge needed to carry on a homosexual relationship at the turn of the century, but are just as applicable to adultery today. I'm sure, too, Byron wrote* So, we'll go no more a-roving *with such a situation in mind. Henry King, being a bishop, probably didn't. But his lines are just as suitable:*

> So, we'll go no more a-roving
>    So late into the night,
> Though the heart be still as loving,
>    And the moon be still as bright.
>
> For the sword outwears its sheath,
>    And the soul wears out the breast,
> And the heart must pause to breathe,
>    And love itself have rest.
>
> Though the night be made for loving
>    And the day returns too soon,
> Yet we'll go no more a-roving
>    By the light of the moon.

*So, we'll go no more a-roving,*
Lord Byron

> We that did nothing study but the way
> To love each other, with which thoughts the day
> Rose with delight to us, and with them set,
> Must learn the hateful art, how to forget.

*The Surrender*, Henry King

# Breaking Up

George Meredith wrote Modern Love in 1862. But it, too, is as relevant today. A long poem, it is a tragedy of married love that starts passionately, then gives way to jealousy and misery, and finally to the separation of a hopelessly ill-matched pair. I have chosen two favourite passages. The first, which actually comes later in the poem, seems to sum up the amount of agony that is expended in marriage for so little: symbolized by the huge waves pounding on the shore that make so little impression on the sand. The second stanza describes those occasional blessed moments of happiness a couple is suddenly granted together, even in moments of intense misery.

Thus piteously Love closed what he begat:
The union of this ever-diverse pair!
These two were rapid falcons in a snare.
Condemned to do the flitting of a bat.
Lovers beneath the singing sky of May,
They wandered once; clear as the dew on flowers:
But they fed not on the advancing hours:
Their hearts held cravings for the buried day.
Then each applied to each that fatal knife,
Deep questioning, which probes to endless dole.
Ah, what a dusty answer gets the soul
When hot for certainties in this our life! —
In tragic hints here see what evermore
Moves dark as yonder midnight ocean's force,
Thundering like ramping hosts of warrior horse,
To throw that faint thin line upon the shore!

•

We saw the swallows gathering in the sky,
And in the osier-isle we heard them noise.
We had not to look back on summer joys,
Or forward to a summer of bright dye.
But in the largeness of the evening earth
Our spirits grew as we went side by side.
The hour became her husband and my bride.
Love, that had robbed us so, thus blessed our dearth!
The pilgrims of the year waxed very low
In multitudinous chatterings, as the flood
Full brown came from the West, and like pale blood
Expanded to the upper crimson cloud.
Love that had robbed us of immortal things,
This little moment mercifully gave,
Where I have seen across the twilight wave
The swan sail with her young beneath her wings.

from *Modern Love*, George Meredith

*T. S. Eliot married twice, the second time very happily. Perhaps this is why he writes so understandingly about marriage breaking up. In this passage from* The Cocktail Party, *the Unidentified Guest talks to Edward whose wife just walked out. When my husband was utterly distraught after his first wife left him, my father-in-law sent him these lines. He found them a great consolation.*

*Unidentified Guest:* The one thing to do
  Is to do nothing. Wait.
*Edward:* Wait!
  But waiting is the one thing impossible
  Besides don't you see that it makes me ridiculous?
*Unidentified Guest:* It will do you no harm to find yourself
  ridiculous.
  Resign yourself to be the fool you are.
  That's the best advice that I can give you.
*Edward:* But how can I wait, not knowing what I am waiting
  for?

Shall I say to my friends, 'My wife has gone away?'
And they answer 'Where?' and I say 'I don't know;'
And they say, 'But when will she be back?'
And I reply 'I don't know that she *is* coming back.'
And they ask 'But what are you going to do?'
And I answer 'Nothing.' They will think me mad.
Or simply contemptible.
*Unidentified Guest:* All to the good.
You will find that you survive humiliation.
And that's an experience of incalculable value.

*The Cocktail Party*, T. S. Eliot

*Finally here are three lines from T. S. Eliot's* Ash Wednesday *which I find a great comfort when I am eaten up by jealousy or misery.*

Suffer us not to mock ourselves with falsehood
Teach us to care, and not to care
Teach us to sit still

from *Ash Wednesday*, T. S. Eliot

♥
♥ ♥
♥

---

## Old Age

*The lover begins to grow old. But in C. Day Lewis's marvellous poem,* The Album, *he still goes on loving one beautiful girl, sadly watching her grow up, recognize her sexual power, take a multitude of lovers and finally be destroyed by them. When I had a boyfriend who was playing around, the lines I used to say over and over to myself were:*

> Give not to those charming desperadoes
> What was made to be mine.

*The word 'desperado' has such a casual pillaging quality about it.*

I see you, a child
in a garden sheltered for buds and playtime,
Listening as if beguiled
By a fancy beyond your years and the flowering maytime.
The print is faded: soon there will be
No trace of that pose enthralling,
Nor visible echo of my voice distantly calling
'Wait! Wait for me!'

Then I turn the page
To a girl who stands like a questioning iris
By the waterside, at an age
That asks every mirror to tell what the heart's desire is.
The answer she finds in that oracle stream
Only time could affirm or disprove,
Yet I wish I was there to venture a warning, 'Love
Is not what you dream.'

Next you appear
As if garlands of wild felicity crowned you –
Courted, caressed, you wear
Like immortelles the lovers and friends around you.
'They will not last you, rain or shine,
They are but straws and shadows,'
I cry: 'Give not to those charming desperadoes
What was made to be mine.'

One picture is missing –
The last. It would show me a tree stripped bare
By intemperate gales, her amazing
Noonday of blossom spoilt which promised so fair.
Yet, scanning those scenes at your heyday taken,
I tremble, as one who must view
In the crystal a doom he could never deflect – yes, I too
Am fruitlessly shaken.

I close the book;
But the past slides out of its leaves to haunt me
And it seems, wherever I look,
Phantoms of irreclaimable happiness taunt me.
Then I see her, petalled in new-bloom hours,
Beside me – 'All you love most there
Has blossomed again,' she murmurs, 'all that you missed
    there
Has grown to be yours.'

*The Album*, C. Day Lewis

*Yeats' life was blighted by his unrequited love for Maud Gonne, and yet this love inspired some of his finest poetry. In this lovely sonnet, with its agonizing last lines, Yeats shows that her beauty was even more heartrending as she grew older:*

One that is ever kind said yesterday:
'Your well-beloved's hair has threads of grey,
And little shadows come about her eyes;
Time can but make it easier to be wise,

Though now it seems impossible, and so
All that you need is patience.' Heart cries no,
I have not a crumb of comfort, not a grain.
Time can but make her beauty over again:
Because of that great nobleness of hers
The fire that stirs about her, when she stirs,
Burns but more clearly. O she had not these ways
When all the wild summer was in her gaze.

Oh heart! Oh heart! if she'd but turn her head
You'd know the folly of being comforted.

*The Folly of Being Comforted*, W. B. Yeats

*As beautiful people grow old, one is always hoping they'll go off a bit, and lose their pulling power.*

*'Hasn't she lost her looks,' I say hopefully about some havoc-maker who caused me sleepless nights of jealousy back in the sixties.*

*'Has she?' says my husband in surprise, 'I thought she looked fine.' If one needs reassurance therefore, don't fall for young lovers, but stick to the people who loved you when you were young, and who with luck don't notice the ravages of time:*

To me, fair friend, you never can be old,
For as you were when first your eye I ey'd,
Such seems your beauty still. Three winters cold
Have from the forests shook three summers' pride,
Three beauteous springs to yellow autumn turn'd
In process of the seasons have I seen,
Three April perfumes in three hot Junes burn'd
Since first I saw you fresh, which yet are green.

from *Sonnet CIV*, William Shakespeare

*To the young, the old seem quite incapable of love, or, even worse, sexual desire. When I was fourteen, I thought anyone over twenty was positively decrepit. Hamlet storms at his mother:*

You cannot call it love, for at your age
The hey-day in the blood is tame, it's humble
And waits upon the judgment.

*Thomas Hardy denied this. It is just as possible, he felt, to be
consumed by passion when one is old.*

I look into my glass,
And view my wasting skin,
And say, 'Would God it came to pass
My heart had shrunk as thin!'

For then, I, undistrest
By hearts grown cold to me,
Could lonely wait my endless rest
With equanimity.

But Time, to make me grieve,
Part steals, lets part abide;
And shakes this fragile frame at eve
With throbbings of noontide.

*I Look Into My Glass,*
Thomas Hardy

*Some women are terrified of growing old, and fortunately some
men appreciate this. John Freeman, for example, pleads with
the years to treat his beloved gently:*

Be kind to her
O Time.
She is too much afraid of you
    Because yours is a land unknown,
    Wintry, and dark and lone.

'Tis not for her
To pass
Boldly upon your roadless waste.
    Roads she loves, and the bright ringing
    Of quick heels, and clear singing.

She is afraid
Of Time,
Forty to seventy sadly fearing . . .
    O, all those unknown years,
    And these sly, stoat-like fears!

Shake not on her
Your snows,
But on the rich, the proud, the wise
    Who have that to make them glow
    With warmth beneath the snow.

If she grow old
At last,
Be it yet unknown to her; that she
    Not until her last prayer is prayed
    May whisper, 'I am afraid!'

                    *To End Her Fear*, John Freeman

*She might have been consoled by the following poems from John Donne and Philip Oakes who display a great tenderness and love towards older women:*

No Spring, nor Summer beauty hath such grace,
As I have seen in one Autumnal face.

                    *The Autumnal*, John Donne

You are veined like a leaf.
Babies have tenderized your breasts,
Munching the tissues with their bony gums.
    Your fingers are scored
By chopping knives, the oven door,
Hot fat, and rose thorns.
    No one would call
You beautiful. Your hair is brindled
By time and weather,
    Your skin is foxed

Like a first edition. You show
Distinct signs of wear and tear.
   Cats sleep in your lap,
Children come to have their noses blown.
You keep secrets like a strong box.
   You are not for special
Occasions, but for everyday. You have
The virtues of denim, wholemeal, and worsted.
   You are durable,
You bring words out of storage,
And on your lips they do not sound strange.
   Love, duty, service:
Sturdier than slipwear, but with the same
Patina, the same hair-line cracks.
   In your house, though,
They are for use, and not display.
They are not allowed to gather dust.
   You are not one
For ornaments. They break easily
Or get in the way.
   You prefer shelves, tables,
Lives to be uncluttered. Without distraction
Wood shows its grain, glass its sparkle.
   You are happiest
When nothing goes remarked, and celebration
Is the act itself.
   You are patient with people,
And implements, you can tie knots,
And start engines. Vegetables grow for you.
   I will not praise you, beyond saying
That you are able, amiable, and welcome.
You meet all guarantees. You are as promised.

                    *Guarantee*, Philip Oakes

*While Wordsworth almost makes one look forward to growing old. Much better than his picture of one surrounded by babies:*

> Thou, while thy babies around thee cling,
> Shalt show us how divine a thing
> A Woman may be made.
>
> . . . .
>
> But an old age, serene and bright,
> And lovely as a Lapland night,
> Shall lead thee to thy grave.

from *To a Young Lady*,
William Wordsworth

*Compensation*

*One of the compensations of old age, and the taming of the blood, is that one spends less time worrying about the opposite sex, and has more time to love and enjoy other things. The next four poems are about this enjoyment. As he grows older the Englishman tends to appreciate the countryside more and more, knowing he has fewer and fewer years to do so. Wordsworth's greatest poem Tintern Abbey is all about loving Nature, and how the obsessive aching adoration of the boy gives way to the calm reflective understanding of the mature man. In a way, it seems to be the right way for love for someone of the opposite sex to develop.*

> I cannot paint
> What then I was. The sounding cataract
> Haunted me like a passion: the tall rock,
> The mountain, and the deep and gloomy wood,
> Their colours and their forms, were then to me
> An appetite; a feeling and a love,
> That had no need of a remoter charm,
> By thought supplied, nor any interest
> Unborrowed from the eye. – That time is past,
> And all its aching joys are now no more,
> And all its dizzy raptures. Not for this
> Faint I, nor mourn nor murmur; other gifts
> Have followed; for such loss, I would believe,
> Abundant recompense. For I have learned
> To look on nature, not as in the hour
> Of thoughtless youth; but hearing oftentimes
> The still, sad music of humanity,
> Nor harsh nor grating, though of ample power

To chasten and subdue. And I have felt
A presence that disturbs me with the joy
Of elevated thoughts; a sense sublime
Of something far more deeply interfused,
Whose dwelling is the light of setting suns,
And the round ocean and the living air
And the blue sky, and in the mind of man.

from *Tintern Abbey*,
William Wordsworth

*Wordsworth's friend, Coleridge, understood how loving all creatures great and small helps you to a better life and a better understanding of your fellow men. One of the most poignant moments in* The Ancient Mariner *is when the Mariner, cursed for his crime against Creation: killing the albatross, suddenly without thinking blesses the water snakes for their beauty. Immediately the albatross falls from his neck:*

Beyond the shadow of the ship,
I watched the water snakes:
They moved in tracks of shining white,
And when they reared, the elfish light
Fell off in hoary flakes.

Within the shadow of the ship,
I watched their rich attire:
Blue, glossy green, and velvet black
They coiled and swam; and every track
Was a flash of golden fire.

O happy living things! no tongue
Their beauty might declare:
A spring of love gushed from my heart,
And I blessed them unaware:
Sure my kind saint took pity on me,
And I blessed them unaware:

The selfsame moment I could pray;
And from my neck so free
The Albatross fell off, and sank
Like lead into the sea.

from *The Ancient Mariner*,
Samuel Taylor Coleridge

*Having shivered on so many touchlines myself, I know how obsessed the British male is with playing games, and how much the sporting heroes of his youth meant to him. They were Gods worshipped at a time of hope, when the world seemed young. Francis Thompson's poem* At Lords, *combines this love of heroes with a nostalgic craving for one's own home ground. A Northerner living in the South, he dreams of the great Lancashire cricketing stars of his boyhood. Coming from Yorkshire myself, and having often gone to the Roses match between the white rose of Yorkshire, and the red rose of Lancashire – I hero-worshipped Hutton and Willie Watson – I can never read this poem without a lump coming into my throat:*

It is little I repair to the matches of the Southron folk,
    Though my own red roses there may blow;
It is little I repair to the matches of the Southron folk,
    Though the red roses crest the caps, I know.
For the field is full of shades as I near the shadowy coast,
And a ghostly batsman plays to the bowling of a ghost,
And I look through my tears on a soundless-clapping host,
    As the run stealers flicker to and fro,
    To and fro: –
Oh my Hornby and my Barlow long ago!

*At Lords*, Francis Thompson

*Finally in this section, we have George Herbert's poem* The Flower, *showing that even after great loss and intense unhappiness, the heart recovers, and its owner is able to pick up the pieces:*

Who would have thought my shrivelled heart
Could have recovered greenness? It was gone
   Quite under ground, as flowers depart
To see their mother-root when they have blown;
   Where they together
   All the hard weather,
Dead to the world, keep house unknown.

These are thy wonders, Lord of Power,
Killing and quickening, bringing down to hell
   And up to heaven in an hour;
Making a chiming of a passing-bell.
   We say amiss,
   This or that is:
Thy word is all, if we could spell.
. . . .
   And now in age I bud again,
After so many deaths I live and write;
   I once more smell the dew and rain,
And relish versing: O my only Light,
   It cannot be
   That I am he
On whom thy tempests fell all night.

from *The Flower*, George Herbert

# Death

We come to death. In old age, perhaps, a happy marriage is most appreciated because it is continuously dogged by a fear that one of the partners may die. Michael Drayton wrote these lovely lines the night before he died:

> Soe well I love thee, as without thee I
> Love Nothing. If I might chuse, I'd rather die
> Than bee one day debarde thy company.

Vita Sackville-West wrote equally tenderly to Harold Nicolson, but alas it was she who died first and he never really recovered from the loss:

I was always well trained not to manage you, I scarcely dare to arrange the collar of your greatcoat, unless you ask me to. I think that is really the basis of our marriage, apart from our deep love for each other, for we have never interfered with each other, and strangely enough, never been jealous of each other. And now, in our advancing age, we love each other more deeply than ever, and also more agonizingly, since we see the inevitable end. It is not nice to know that one of us must die before the other.

Vita Sackville-West writing to Harold Nicolson

Now three poems about facing up to death. Bishop King, being of a stoical nature, had, after his wife died, to face the grey dreariness of life alone but he couldn't wait to join her. Sir Albertus Moreton's wife didn't try very hard to go on living. Chaucer, on the other hand, is haunted by the loneliness of the grave.

Sleep on my Love, in thy cold bed,
Never to be disquieted!
My last good night! Thou wilt not wake
Till I thy fate shall overtake:
Till age, or grief, or sickness must
Marry my body to that dust
It so much loves; and fill the room
My heart keeps empty in thy Tomb.
Stay for me there; I will not fail
To meet thee in that hollow Vale.
And think not much of my delay;
I am already on the way,
And follow thee with all the speed
Desire can make, or sorrows breed.
Each minute is a short degree,
And ev'ry houre a step towards thee.
At night when I betake to rest,
Next morn I rise nearer my West
Of life, almost by eight houres saile,
Than when sleep breath'd his drowsie gale.

. . . .

Tis true, with shame and grief I yield,
Thou like the Vann first took'st the field,
And gotten hast the victory
In thus adventuring to dy
Before me, whose more years might crave
A just precedence in the grave.
But heark! My Pulse like a soft Drum
Beats my approach, tell Thee I come;
And slow howere my marches be,
I shall at last sit down by Thee.

The thought of this bids me go on,
And wait my dissolution
With hope and comfort. Dear (forgive
The crime) I am content to live

Divided, with but half a heart,
Till we shall meet and never part.

from *The Exequy*, Henry King

He first deceas'd; she for a little tri'd
To live without him; lik'd it not and di'd!

*Death of Sir Albertus Moreton's Wife*,
Sir Henry Wotton

What is this world? What asketh men to have
Now with his love, now in his colde grave
Allone, with-outen any companye.

from *The Knighte's Tale*,
Geoffrey Chaucer

*Often, when we're unhappily in love, fate plays a cruel trick by
making us suddenly think we see the loved one in a crowd, so
we bound forward – all expectation – only to realize we're
mistaken. The subconscious played an equally cruel trick on
Milton. After his wife died, he dreamed she was alive:*

Methought I saw my late espoused Saint
    Brought to me like Alcestis from the grave,
    Whom Joves great Son to her glad Husband gave,
    Rescu'd from death by force though pale and faint.
Mine as whom washt from spot of child-bed taint,
    Purification in the old Law did save,
    And such, as yet once more I trust to have
    Full sight of her in Heaven without restraint,
Came vested all in white, pure as her mind:
    Her face was vail'd, yet to my fancied sight,
    Love, sweetness, goodness, in her person shin'd
So clear, as in no face with more delight.
    But O as to embrace me she enclin'd,
    I wak'd, she fled, and day brought back my night.

*Sonnet XIX*, John Milton

*Now a poem by Thomas Hardy. This is his great farewell to love, written after his first wife died, and when the poet himself was over seventy. Here he expresses the lover's innate belief that he and his beloved are immortalized by the intensity of their love — more intense than anyone's before or since:*

As I drive to the junction of lane and highway,
    And the drizzle bedrenches the waggonette,
I look behind at the fading byway,
    And see on its slope, now glistening wet,
        Distinctly yet

Myself and a girlish form benighted
    In dry March weather. We climb the road
Beside a chaise. We had just alighted
    To ease the sturdy pony's load
        When he sighed and slowed.

What we did as we climbed, and what we talked of
    Matters not much, nor to what it led, –
Something that life will not be balked of
    Without rude reason till hope is dead,
        And feeling fled.

It filled but a minute. But was there ever
    A time of such quality, since or before,
In that hill's story? To one mind never,
    Though it has been climbed, foot-swift, foot-sore,
        By thousands more.

Primaeval rocks form the road's steep border,
    And much have they faced there, first and last,
Of the transitory in Earth's long order;
    But what they record in colour and cast
        Is that we two passed.

And to me, though Time's unflinching rigour,
    In mindless rote, has ruled from sight

The substance now, one phantom figure
   Remains on the slope, as when that night
    Saw us alight.

I look and see it there, shrinking, shrinking.
   I look back at it amid the rain
For the very last time; for my sand is sinking,
   And I shall traverse old love's domain
    Never again.

            *At Castle Boterel*, Thomas Hardy

*We end with another poem by Hardy. When I first read it at school I thought it was unutterably flat and dreary, and was sharply and justifiably reprimanded by my English mistress. She pointed out that in simple, beautiful language, it expresses the great truth that, although dynasties may fall, and wars destroy, the important things – love between man and woman, growing enough food to eat, and burning the weeds that threaten the crops – will go on forever.*

Only a man harrowing clods
   In a slow silent walk
With an old horse that stumbles and nods
   Half asleep as they stalk,

Only thin smoke without flame
   From the heaps of couch grass;
Yet this will go onward the same
   Though Dynasties pass.

Yonder a maid and her wight
   Come whispering by:
War's annals will cloud into night
   Ere their story die.

      *In the Time of 'the Breaking of Nations'*,
                Thomas Hardy

# Index

*Romance, intrigue, adventure – it's all here
in these unputdownable Penguins*

# The Feast of All Saints
## Anne Rice

In the raw, sensual and legendary city of New Orleans before the Civil War; amongst the waterfronts, the slave markets and the quadroon ballrooms lived the *gens de couleur*, a fierce and proud people, neither black nor white, but caught between the two – free and yet not free.

Out of this race came Marcel, the mesmeric copper-skinned youth, adored by all yet dreaming of distant cultures, and his sister Marie, who longed for love and marriage in a world ready to sell her to the highest bidder.

Exotic and exciting, the author of the bestselling *Interview with the Vampire* has written a novel as colourful and sensuous as the old French Quarter itself.

# Manchu
## Robert Elegant

The big bestseller from the author of *Dynasty* – it'll spellbind and enthrall you to the very last page! The year is 1628, and the fabulous court of the Ming is secretly penetrated by the Jesuits and assaulted by the fierce and terrible Manchu. Here we meet Francis Arrowsmith, an Englishman and exiled Jesuit turned soldier-of-fortune.

Delving back through the shifting sands of time, Robert Elegant recreates the opulence of the Chinese courts, the swift savagery of the wars, the porcelain eroticism of the women and the last embattled days of the doomed Ming dynasty.

# Who's On First
### *William F. Buckley, Jr.*

*TIME:* The Cold War
*PLACE:* Paris, Budapest, Washington, D C, Stockholm, Moscow
*SECRET AGENT:* Young irresistible Blackford Oakes of the CIA
*ASSIGNMENT:* Win the satellite space race with the Soviets

Enter master agent Rufus, CIA Director Allen Dulles, former Secretary of State Dean Acheson, and Tamara, a beautiful Hungarian freedom fighter. His mission is complicated by the President, the US Navy, a K G B area chief, and the alluring Sally, who loves him, hates his work.

The Buckley tension, wit, ingenuity and high drama show why, in his class, he's first.

# Russian Hide-and-Seek
### *Kingsley Amis*

Amis's brilliant and deadly new comedy set in twenty-first century England ruled by the Russians.

Looking for kicks, our hero, the dashing young cavalry officer Alexander Petrovsky moves into an affair with the insatiable, big-breasted wife of the Deputy Director of Security, and on to a dangerous flirtation with counter-revolutionary politics. In attempting to give England back to the English, he's unwittingly joined a game of Russian hide-and-seek . . .

'Amis has emerged triumphant' – *Daily Mail*